SPIRITUAL GEMS OF TRUTH

Inspired by

Sebastian and Mabbr

Written by

Barbara Harvey

Teaching messages of enlightenment for daily readings or spontaneous inspirational support for circumstances of daily life.

Published 2006 by arima publishing

www.arimapublishing.com

ISBN 1 84549 149 1
ISBN 978 1 84549 149 9

Printed and bound in the United Kingdom

Typeset in Garamond 11/14

Swirl is an imprint of arima publishing.

arima publishing
ASK House, Northgate Avenue
Bury St Edmunds, Suffolk IP32 6BB
t: (+44) 01284 700321

www.arimapublishing.com

I dedicate this book to God and Spirit.

ACKNOWLEDGEMENTS

My thanks go to my husband Brian, to Darren my son and to my daughter, Zena, for their patience, love and support,

to Pauline Lee and Jim and Grace Smith for their healings and guidance, and for Jim's sponsorship for retyping the text to help the book come to fruition,

to Mary and Peter MacEchenary and Shirley Olive for inviting me to participate in development circles and courses,

and to Dr. Margaret Teggin (Magi) for editing the book and finding a publisher.

CONTENTS

FOREWORD

It was in 1995 that my wife Grace and I first met Barbara.

We had called at her home in the hamlet of Juniper Hill in north Oxfordshire, in response to her request for spiritual healing to help her with her M.E. symptoms. This was the first of a number of visits to her home over the following years to help her cope with her illness.

We were on about our third visit when Barbara asked me, 'How did you know that you had the gift of spiritual healing?'

I explained to her that Grace and I were members of the Spiritualist Churches at Banbury, Witney and North Oxford, and that we had been told by various visiting speakers that we had the gift of healing if we should choose to develop it. We did this by sitting in development circles and the healing gift developed.

Barbara expressed interest in what we had told her and in due course she attended the churches. Visiting speakers told her that she had the gift of mediumship if she wished to develop it. Barbara knew this was what she wanted to do. She joined development circles and trained in various ways and her gift developed, until now she regularly serves in churches and writes lovely words of philosophy through her guide Sebastian and poems and prayers from Mabbr.

It was not until 1998 when Barbara showed me what she had been writing that I realised the wisdom that was there and that this was a gift that needed to be shared with the world in general. Although it was possible to get the writings typed up there was no funding available to get an electronic version or to get it published, but later Barbara said to me then,

'I'm getting my first book published- will you write the Foreword for me?'

I was of course delighted to be able to do so, since I had been there at the beginning of her development so to speak.

I hope you enjoy the book and the wonderful truths so simply written therein.

God Bless you dear Barbara in your work for your fellow man.

Jim Smith
Summer 2006

Spiritual Healer
North Oxford Church.

INTRODUCTION

How I Came into the Spiritualist Church

On 21st December 1994 I was struck down with M.E. (Myalgic Encephalomyelitis). My G.P. prescribed only painkillers and told me to rest, which was about all I could do for 23 hours a day.

On one of my better mornings I went to Brackley Post Office and bumped into a former work colleague. She suggested I try spiritual healing with a lady called Pauline Lee who lived in Brackley. I was sceptical but booked and went along for my first healing session in May 1995. I found it gave me a pleasant and relaxing feeling, which provided relief from the pain, albeit short-term.

I continued to go once, sometimes twice a week. One week, as I lay on the healing table, I suddenly saw Elvis Presley very clearly and laughed, thinking I was imagining things. I told Pauline who said that another lady she'd had for healing had said the same. After that occasion, each time I was receiving healing I saw vivid colours all around me and I once saw a beautiful golden healing angel leaning over me in a prayer position.

Pauline suggested I attend a spiritualist church, which at that time I put to one side, thinking that it would be full of strange people with strange beliefs.

In September 1995 Pauline was on holiday and I was in a lot of pain and unable to sleep or rest sufficiently, when I came across an article on healing in 'Woman's Own' magazine. This contained a contact number for those interested in help. I rang this number as I was in a lot of pain and feeling very depressed. The number put me in contact with Jim and Grace Smith from Summertown Church. They came to give me healing the very next day and, from then on, I was receiving healing from Jim and Grace once a week and also once a week from Pauline.

One day Jim suggested that if ever I was interested, I should come along to Banbury Church meetings on a Thursday evening as they were always there and I might find it enjoyable.

Well, late in November 1995, my husband was watching football on TV and I was bored, so I thought I would try this spiritualist church in Banbury, which at the time, held its meetings in the Quaker Meeting House. Very apprehensively I went in to find very friendly people and a warm, comfortable atmosphere. The second time I went I received a very accurate message from my father, and the medium also suggested that a development circle would be the right thing to join. That evening I was also aware, even though I had my eyes shut, of a lady, dressed very smartly and holding a prayer book, standing in front of me. When I opened my eyes she had gone, but each time I closed them, I saw her again.

Jim told me what was happening... that my third eye had opened and I was seeing a Quaker lady who often visited the Old Meeting House. He also suggested that I should sit in circle to develop further if the opportunity arose.

It wasn't until March 1996 that I saw Mary Machreary (who used to be Mary Urp) work at the church, and she also suggested a circle. So, after the service, I spoke to her and she invited me to her small home circle.

Mary and her husband Peter gave me my first chance to sit in circle for spiritual development. I have many happy memories of the year I sat with them and two other circle members. Then I felt I had to move on, thanked Mary for all her teachings, and took a short rest from circle work. I was feeling much more uplifted and coping better with my M.E., but I was still having to lie down to rest a lot each day, so I would meditate for long periods of time each day when I was unable to sleep.

Shirley Olive was at Banbury Church in June 1996 and mentioned that she was starting a new open circle on a Monday night if anyone was interested. This was at her teaching centre, *The White Dove Lodge* at Witney.

I have a lot to thank Shirley for. For giving me the opportunity to learn and work with Spirit at the centre in circle, and also on platform when we worked as a group. Then later she gave me individual bookings. She has passed on a great deal of knowledge to me and others and we are good friends now.

I took a Mediumship Manual course with Shirley for two years from September 1997 to September 1999. At the same time I took the Greater World Foundation Study course from September 1997 to 21 September 1998, thinking I would go on to take their Mediumship course. However I was advised by several mediums to stay neutral in my work and not to join any organisation.

I sat in circle with Shirley for seven years until December 2003, making a total of eight years in circle. Now my guides and helpers are still teaching me and I have a lot to learn. For as I learn more, I realise just how little I really know. I find the spiritual way of life very strengthening, giving me greater faith in God, Ascended Masters and all the angels who are constantly working for us and supporting us. We only need to ask for help and it is given.

The inspirational writing *(two articles published in **Insight**, Autumn 2004 – Ed.)*, started in 2nd June 1998, and they have also taught me a lot about life and about myself.

I have many people to thank for support and teaching on my pathway, and probably the most supportive throughout my illness and spiritual awakening are my husband Brian, daughter Zena and son Darren. Although Zena is the only one who believes as I do, my husband is just beginning to show an interest but is still very doubting about God.

So, this is my challenge: to help give Brian and others like him, sharing the knowledge and continuing proof to awaken him to truth, love and Spirit. Ultimately it is up to each individual to find their own proof as we all have free will on our pathways, and I can only answer questions the way I understand the answers. I do not know everything, as we here on Earth are learning constantly.

Hopefully my story will encourage others on the way to enlightenment and service to 'all that is'. It is not easy, nor does it happen overnight for most of us. We must have a willingness to learn and perhaps the hardest of all, patience.

Barbara Harvey

SPIRITUAL GEMS OF TRUTH

LOVE

'Love makes the world go round'. This is one of the truest things ever said. Without love the world would have been destroyed time, and time again. Fighting is an unnecessary evil caused by negative thoughts. Thoughts are living things, just as prayers are living and doing good. Negativity brings destruction, sorrow, despair, fear, heartache, bereavement, sadness, greed, poverty, loneliness, war.

Think of love. What a difference it makes to all. Happiness, compassion, warmth, hope, positive thoughts, peace-giving, respect, joy, fullness of heart and love are all conditions for a thriving population. Think of all the different types of love there are. All are equally good. Here are some to think about:

Love of life itself.
Mother love.
Father love.
Love from a child to its parents.
Love that forms from lust of two lovers into a love that lasts for years and years.
Love of friendship.
Love of your animal companions.
Love of nature, plants and trees.
Love of a hobby.
Love of work.
Love of food and drink.
Love of material things.

We could go on and on, the list is endless. But the love of mankind for one another is so important, even if you don't like the other person. You should love them as a fellow human, a fellow spirit who, like you, is also a tiny part of God. We all carry that Christ light within us. The living Christ Spirit, every man, animal, plant, insect, every one of God's creations. We are all part of the whole ONE.

Treat one another with respect and love. Offer a helping hand or a shoulder to cry on in times of need. Give time, a listening ear, compassion, warmth, understanding and give love. There is nothing more rewarding than that real warmth from the soul.

An open heart is love. You will find the more you give out, the more will be returned to you, tenfold. You will be a very rich person, as love is the very essence of life, enriching the lives of all that embrace it, giving a greater inner peace to all.

Remember, treat everyone, and everything, with kindness, compassion, love, respect, understanding, in other words, as you yourself would want to be treated. The One

Great Power, which created the cosmos, universe and all we know, freely gave His love to all. Creation itself was brought about by Love. The One who loves you most of all, the One true Great Spirit, God, created all we know, with Love.

Remember the Great Mother/Father God, and give daily thanks for all your blessings and pass on the essence of life itself, LOVE.

EXTRA SENSORY PERCEPTION

Extra Sensory Perception, (E.S.P.), or information from the external world by means of sensory perception, is one of the things developed in mediumship by many mediums around the world. Some people do not understand this form of mediumship, as it differs in the way it manifests itself from mediumship on the working platform which is mental mediumship.

Mental mediumship happens in a direct way, where the guide has entered the aura of the medium, and is able to transmit thought directly into the medium's consciousness. The thought flow from spirit goes directly into speech through the medium, without any conscious effort to create the address themselves. The Spirit projects the thought intention into speech, and the thought flow is usually vigorous and continuous. The medium simply has to speak the words given by the guide, taking care not to interrupt the process in any way. If this happens, the direct link with spirit will be severed, resulting in the medium being completely lost for words, finding that the address is over and they have to sit down. So if any words come out wrong, or do not make sense to you, do not try to attempt to correct them, as they will probably be corrected somewhere along with the speech by the guide. This is a form of very light trance mediumship where the medium usually speaks in his or her usual voice, and appears to be completely aware of what they are saying. In fact they are listening to themselves speak, without any conscious effort to create the address themselves.

Sometimes a medium is given the words in advance of the platform work. This is a way of getting them up on the platform, even if they are still unsure of themselves. Spirit has ways and means of encouraging people onto the platform, so that the new medium can get their message across.

A light trance can be is very subtle, and even the mediums are at times unaware that they are not directly in control of what is being said. In any form of trance the words flow on and on. For this reason alone, it is extremely important for the medium up on the platform to feel confident enough to allow themselves to be an empty vehicle for the message to come through. In faith, they give themselves to spirit, so that they can speak as directed, not even correcting any mispronounced word, for any such alteration could break off contact with the guide.

This light trance work is very similar to automatic writing, the difference being that the hand is used rather than the voice. The medium feels a compulsion to pick up a pen and to write the intuitive thought flow instead of speaking it. S/he watches the thoughts being written into words and phrases. Automatic writing is often given to mediums who do not yet feel confident enough to stand up in front of a group of people.

Sometimes a medium reads a previously inspired speech. People may feel they have been cheated out of a direct inspirational speech when they see the medium reading their address, but this is just another way in which spirit helps mediums to stand up and deliver the messages they want you to know.

DEVELOPMENT

To develop spiritual gifts, as many of you wish to do, it is far better to develop them slowly. This way you can absorb the important signs, symbols and messages.

Spirit likes to work with each person individually. This all takes time and patience, as the channel for any type of Mediumship needs to be cleared. If the Chakras are not spinning in unison, or are blocked, information and healing energies are unable to get through.

Pure diet, sun-ripened fruits, vegetables, pulses and the elixir of life (water) are all important foods for your development. Water is the greatest cleanser and a great energy source. It is also a source of psychic energy, a great sustenance of all life, without it none would exist.

Sun-ripened fruits; vegetables, pulses and water, absorb the natural energies from our sun. The parent plants and trees also absorb the magnetic energy from mother earth. The energy elements of wind and rain have also been captured within these superb natural packages.

A careful diet ensures your earthly bodies absorb the correct nutrition. Then Spirit will have all the correct natural elements flowing through the human channel. Equal amounts of activity and rest are also of great importance as all should be in balance.

It is important that you also feed your mind with correct thoughts, and that you follow this through with correct speech and actions, as the whole of you, mind, body and soul, needs to be in balance. Then development with the highest Guides will be possible.

Keeping company with like-minded people is recommended. This is of great value to the spirit, especially if you sit in meditation together in what you refer to as 'circles'. This way spirit can use the sitters as another energy source for the development of those chosen for service to mankind at that particular time. Simultaneously, the sitters develop ability to reflect and self-analyse, allowing for integration of the whole self.

The importance of prayer must not be forgotten, for this corresponds to your spiritual need for the expression of your inner self to the Great Mother/Father Spirit, whom you call God. This enables one to listen to the divine spark of God, which is in everyone.

Remember, development of spiritual gifts for service to mankind, should never be rushed. You do not need to become a medium to love and help one another. Loving and helping each other is just as important as any other service. Serving one another as God intended is a source of joy and is important for your soul's development.

Remember, service to all God's creation should be given willingly with love and an open heart.

A HELPING HAND

How often have you wished for a helping hand? God offers you all His helping hand. It is up to you whether you accept this help, so freely and lovingly offered to you all.

You all tend to think you know best in all things, not listening in every moment to that inner spark of God within each and everyone of you. Listen. Listen carefully to your inner spark, to your intuition or conscience as you may call it. Just take a little time to sit back from the situation.

Sit quietly. Sit still. Listen to your inner self. Far better decisions will be made in your lives. Problems would not appear like the great mountains you sometimes choose to climb. They will be more like molehills, far easier to overcome.

Guides and helpers are constantly trying to guide your footsteps onto the right pathways of life. Guides and loved ones put the right thoughts into your hearts and minds. Sometimes you pay attention to these ideas, at other times you disregard them and you follow your earthly minds. Consequently you end up in a mess, having to do a lot more work before you can get the desired result.

If only you all followed your hearts more and listened to your inner selves, the Christ Spirit within all of you, then your world's problems would disappear, as only right-thinking would reach fruition. War, famine and greed, would not exist and the world you all pray for, a world of Love and Peace, would be yours.

Let us pray that one day, not too far away, the Christ Light will be awakened in all Mankind, so that your dreams of a beautiful world of love, peace, warmth, shelter and food for all, will be realised.

Remember, if you are unsure of what steps to take in your lives, sit back. Do not rush head strong into the situation. Relax a little. Do not let negative thoughts and emotions of panic, fear, and anxiety take over. Realise that all will come right if you take your time and listen inwardly. "Stay cool" as you say. Listen to your intuition, to your conscience, as this is your true Guide. Do this, and your lives will be much sweeter and more fulfilling for all.

Kindle the flame within your friends and families, by the lives you lead. Listen to your inner God light. Live a life of right thought, so that right action will be taken and your life will be for the good of all on earth.

SPIRITUAL BOOKS

Reading spiritual books is not necessary to become a good spiritualist for the books themselves will not make you a spiritual person, just as going to church regularly will not make you a good Christian, or a good person. Spirituality has to come from within your own heart. You are the one who has to activate your own mind and soul, so that goodness will flow from you, for the good of all of God's creations. You have to really want to serve one another, not wait to receive something in return. Serving each other and all living things, is serving the Great Spirit. This is reward enough.

Books are an excellent way to educate yourself, and to open up your mind to spiritual truths. Learning about the ways that spirit can use you for mediumship, and about how you can help the process by meditation and Christ-like thought, speech and action, is all written in these books for those hungry to learn. Whichever gift God has given you, (i.e. healing, clairvoyance (for seeing), clairaudience (for hearing) and clairsentience (for feeling)), all must be used carefully for the good of all. They are precious gifts from God and should never be misused.

These gifts have been given to you to help you go forward on your spiritual path, growing stronger and more loving as you use your understanding to help others. Learning the basics from books can be helpful, so you can understand what is happening. However, if you have been given the gift of being a channel for the power of spirit to flow and work through you, never assume it is your power. Without Spirit, you could not do such wondrous things.

These gifts have to be used wisely, unselfishly, and humbly, with the intention to help all God's creation. Do not let your ego take over, for the gifts will be taken back just as quickly as they were given. Use these wondrous gifts to serve, heal and comfort one another. Let loved ones in spirit comfort their loved ones on the earth. Proving to them that life is eternal, and that family and friends in spirit are now whole, well, and happy. Demonstrate that there is no such thing as death, that earthly life is but a chapter in your soul growth.

Yes, it is good to read, to enlighten oneself but unconditional love for each another is what makes a good spiritualist. Remember, every loving thing God has created, is a part of the interconnected WHOLE. This includes YOU. All of you are part of each other, so treat everyone as you would wish to be treated.

Used correctly and unselfishly, your connection to spirit will never let you down. Have faith. Serve one another. The happiness and inner peace you receive through this divine service to one another is priceless. Enjoy your lives. Be loving, give freely of yourself. Enjoy service, love and inner peace in your lives.

It is up to you to activate your spirituality and use your knowledge to overcome any negativity you meet in your lives. Your journey of growth is not an easy one, but being loving and giving freely of yourself to serve each other and God, is richly rewarded by the inflow of great love and inner peace that you receive in return. Enjoy life as God intended you to. Being spiritual is something you cannot buy over a counter. It flows from your soul, if only you will let it.

TOLERANCE

Tolerance is extremely challenging, especially when daily life is a little difficult. Try to control your thoughts and actions. Listen carefully to other people, then respond peacefully. This is so important. Tell each other how you feel about any situation that arises, and do listen to different points of view. Your intolerance could be causing a problem. Keep an open mind and keep talking to one another for communication is one of society's life support systems, as is tolerance. Aggressive behaviour and arguing will not solve anything. It will just inflame the situation further. Self discipline is the only way to keep anger under control.

Try to be calm and sensitive to other people's feelings and circumstances. Do not judge. You have no right to be judgmental of another. If there is a disagreement, you must try to make the effort to bring love and peace back to that whole area of your life. Apologise. Everyone is learning on their own life journey. Different circumstances and challenges surround everyone. Always be tolerant of other points of view.

Humanity must co-operate with each other. Always hold everyone in love and peace, especially when there might be conflict. If people do not make this effort as individuals, how can there ever be a chance of global peace? Friends, family, and colleagues can live in love, peace and harmony if everyone is tolerant of each other's situation. If they can't do this, what chance is there for nations to tolerate each other, or for peace on earth?

It is so important to demonstrate love, tolerance, compassion and sensitivity to one another whilst upon the earth plane. Once you have passed to spirit and realise that hurt has been caused to others, it is far more difficult to put things right. Communication between the material world and spirit is not always very easy as the gap between them widens for the people involved. Bitterness can flow towards a person for having caused such pain. Memories will hold the pain of those bitter times, festering away like acid burning into your soul, unless there is forgiveness, compassion and tolerance.

If you pass into spirit without reconciling and forgiving hurtful interactions, the pain may increase so much that it will take a long time to heal the rift between the parties involved. Both sides are injured by such an unfortunate incident. Both sides need to forgive and to be forgiven before healing can occur and they can once again love and care for one another and move along on their journey. This has to be done quickly, otherwise the souls involved will be held back by any bitterness they still hold.

Remember, love one another and be tolerant. No one has the right to control, judge or to force their views upon others. You are all on your own unique spirit journeys of growth. Your earthly lives and characters are part of the earthly lessons you have come to learn. To grow spiritually more Christ-like, live your lives lovingly. Be tolerant. Communicate lovingly. Everyone will find life is sweet as you reach amicable agreements, making your world the peaceful place you all wish it to be.

Remember, what you do to each other will always return to you by universal law.

PASSION

What is Passion? It can be any strongly felt emotion such as love, hate or envy, or a great yearning from within the heart centre. When you are in love, we may say you have an ardent affection or passion to be with that person as much as possible. There is passion for a hobby or the fun aspect of life, like dancing or a sport. Passion can also take the form of an obsession. It can take over your life in one way or another.

God wishes you to have a great passion for all you do whilst here on the earth plane. Enjoy laughter. Enjoy all the experiences. Enjoy. Enjoy.

Yes! A great passion for life, that is what the Great Creator, the Great Spirit has intended for all. A love, a passion for life for all of you, to be enjoyed whilst here, while learning, and finding your own pathways as you learn the way of the Lord. Hopefully, that is what will come about sooner rather than later, after many, many lives. The yearning to learn, to partake and strive to become God-like, in thought, speech and action, that is the passion the Lord hopes you will all eventually reach. For reach it you will, all at different times, depending upon your soul growth, becoming one with the Great Creator Himself, God!

While here on the earth plane, you will have enthusiasm to do this and that, some good, some bad. Some of your actions will take the form of a complete lesson in themselves. Other actions will be harder lessons which you will have to try to learn again and again through life- perhaps through many lives. However, the will of your spirit, will eventually flow through your heavy body mass, and be illuminated with the goodness of the Lord, the God, if only you will let it.

Do not worry what others think or say as you follow your righteous path. You will know within your heart it is the right path for you. When you reach it, let no man turn you away from it, but love life, and enjoy your earth. It is a gift bestowed to all, for all to enjoy. Live life. Be as passionate about it as God intended.

TAKE A LITTLE TIME

Time rules humans in the duration of your life span. Time is the essence of your earthly living, the continuous passage of existence past, present, future.

Here in Spirit, we have no time to worry us. We see all you rush, rush everywhere. Why? Take a little time, enjoy your lives. You have no time to enjoy the simple things of life around and about you on the beautiful planet earth.

Take time, just a little of your time, to look around you. See the beautiful colours of the plant world, the flowers, and the trees. See the beautiful birds, butterflies and animals around you.

Glorious colours are around you. Musical sounds of nature reach your ears, and eyes. Yet you may see and hear nothing of all this wonderment. Do you hear birdsong, rustling leaves, frogs croaking? No, not you, for you are far too busy listening to manmade noises. Noise is all about you, radio waves, television, car noise, machinery noise. All are noises that make you nervous, stressed, ill.

Relax a little. Listen to nature's healing music of bird songs, the whispering leaves of the trees and all these wonderful sounds that are given to sooth your nerves.

You have a vast stretch of time on the earth; you have so much time. Really enjoy your earth. Slow down. You start to rush, rush, rush. You have trouble to quieten the body down, you get what you call, addicted to rushing and hurrying around.

Health comes to those who are still. Who watch and listen. Try to remember that the hurrying and worrying, does you no good. Illness may creep upon you, and then you wonder why.

Harmony is the answer. Balance in all you do. What you eat. How much you work and play and of course, rest.

You constantly ask, 'How do I get and stay well?'
Eat the sun-ripened fruits of the earth, and drink the life giving waters, and balance work and play.

Balance everything in your life, including noise, and peace. Harmony is the key to health for body and soul. Take time for yourself and learn.

TIME

Give time to the lonely, they need someone to talk to and listen to their problems. Let them reminisce, talk about the high spots of their lives, they always wish to share them. The old are wise, they have lived their lives, been through many of the problems you are encountering. Listen to them, give them your time, your attention, learn from them, they have so much they can give to you. Time is one thing the old have to give you, with all their past experiences.

Giving time is very hard for some of you, you think you have no time, you rush and tear around. You all have time. Just try to follow your heart, it will give you all the feelings, telling you how to give that time best. Some seem to give continuously. they have learnt what it is that makes them happy- it is to see others fill with joy. Everyone can give time, love, compassion to all they encounter.

Everyone learns as they tread their pathway. yes, pass on the lessons you have learnt to the young, for teaching them to give of themselves is the most important way, to give time, love, compassion to all, especially the old, sick, lonely. We know the young find it hard to give a little time to listen to you. They believe it doesn't concern them, but soon they will realise you really did know what you spoke about. This gives them the insight they need to learn the art of giving and respecting others.

Give your best at work, rest and play, while you are on the earth. It is what you have come to do. Enjoy your time there. People always assume they need more wealth to be able to give. They do not realise that other things in life are far more important than wealth. To give something of yourself is far better. Yes, clear out your cupboards of clutter you no longer need. Why hold it when charities can use this to help others. Take time, yet again, clear out and to give.

For some it is so very hard to give their time and energy, freely to others, there are so many that need this. Learn to give, it is so rewarding. To take has no such rewards. The feelings, the affections you will feel in return for such a little of your time will be a great reward. Yes, you can all give. You all have lots to give to others. You all have different gifts within yourselves to give in service to your fellow humans. Things you are good at can be passed on to others who will learn when you give them time.

Help each other, earth can be such a difficult place to be at times. Remember everyone can give of themselves. You do not need to be rich in the material sense to be able to give and serve one another. God has given wholly of himself constantly, given love and eternal life to all his children.

Learn in this time you have on this beautiful earth to love yourself and to give yourself time also, then giving others the love and respect that is a part of yourself is so much easier for you.

You all have so very many blessings given to you by your Mother/Father God. Time is just one of them. Live your lives. Enjoy!

WORK

Work! We all have our work to do, some in the home, some in the work place. All work is service, and all service is important. It transfers your energy, as you express it in your daily work. Exert effort. Perform your daily tasks effectively. All you accomplish is to your own advantage. If you always give of your best in all tasks, directing physical, mental effort always, it is the most you can do. Do not reproach yourself for things that may happen around you. Some things are totally out of your hands. You are not the only one who has problems that arise. I will not speak of specific conditions, as all are worrying, however large or small to the person in a quandary. Take heart, knowing that all your friends, family and guides do all they can in the spirit world to help you. They smooth your pathways as much as they are able. The dilemma, when looked back upon, was hardly ever as bad as expected. You managed to come through as always.

We here, ask you to keep your faith. Father God knows of all your predicaments, large or small, however trivial they may seem to others. He understands your concern and lends a guiding hand to help. Everything you come across on earth is a learning opportunity relevant to your personal schooling. Difficult situations are all problems that have been discussed with you in spirit before you went to earth. You have all heard many tell that you have chosen your lives on earth. It is true, you are the only one who knows how much you can take as an individual, although at the time, while living through the experiences, you have no recall of the lessons you agreed to learn.

Take heart, fellow spirit. Enjoy your life. All is never as bad as it seems. You will realise this when you return home, and look back over the work you have accomplished and the pains you bore mentally and physically to do your utmost best, in the circumstances around you. Do not despair. All have their problems. Some do not show them as much as others, but they worry just as much within. We see this here in spirit. It is all worthwhile. Not one of you on earth wanted an easy time, for if you had, then you would learn nothing. It is all worthwhile. Just do your best. No one will judge you when you return home for there is no judge and jury, as many fear. Many of you are so afraid to die, as you call it, and face your Maker. Your Creator loves you. No form of punishment will be given to you. You each have the spirit within you, your own God part. You will judge how well you accomplished your assignment on earth yourselves. There is no death, only life eternal for all. There is no terrible punishment awaiting you here in spirit.

Each one of you has to tread every possible way of life. Every possible task will be undertaken by yourselves, throughout your schooling of life. Just do your duty to be a hard worker. Plenty of "elbow grease", I believe you say! It matters not what you do. All work is service to one another, and this is all your Mother/Father God asks of you. Have no fear of the Lord thy God. He is the ever-loving, ever-caring parent of all.

May a blessing be given to you all, for all the work you have agreed to undertake and accomplish. It is all to your own advantage, so you may grow steadily nearer your Mother/Father God, Mighty Spirit, giver of all life.

SPIRIT AND SOUL

Spirit, you all know, is the life force God has given you. It is part of the Great Spirit himself and is a gift of life to you all through his creation. The Great Creator gave you this spirit the moment you were conceived and from that moment on, when you entered the flesh, you started to develop the second part of your true self, your soul.

Without spirit there is no soul. The soul of man carries vast information from the past existences into this life, although he is unaware of them. This is the way God intended. What has past is finished with. The future is the most important part of your life. When you return to spirit all will be clear to you. You will understand why you had no knowledge of your past lives. You are a spirit, the light of God, with a soul. Your earthly life is for you to learn from for your soul to grow nearer to spirit. For this soul growth, you are here on the earth. Each of you has life troubles, lessons which you have to learn from, allowing the soul to grow.

The soul has two parts. One part dies with the body, crumblimg away. The other can live on with spirit, providing the breath of God has been given to it. The soul has no life until the spirit and soul join together. The spirit is the God part of you. Spirit and Soul are the Yin and Yang of the body (male and female).

When spirit and soul grow steadily into one another, the soul is 'christed'. The great light of Christ is born and the spirit has progressed in the soul of man as far as it is able. No more earthly lessons are necessary. The oneness with the Great Spirit is made.

If the soul has been depraved in evil, the two parts will have a great distance between each other. Then spirit and soul must start afresh and development or awakening, takes much longer as they climb up to the light out of the darkness. Until the two are joined, balanced perfectly by goodness, and are illuminated with the Christ light, your lessons must continue.

Without spirit, there is no soul. Without your soul being developed fully, there is no way your spirit can rejoin the one Great Spirit.

Work little ones. Work hard. Your conscience will tell you when you are doing right. Just keep on keeping on, and you will win through to your Father/Mother God's side.

GOODNESS

Goodness comes from the word God-like.

Good comes from God. To be good, is to be God-like in the Father/Mother image. Be God-like in thought, words and actions. In other words, always demonstrate your best, positive qualities, the untainted side of yourselves. It is not easy we know.

Remember, it is God who gives you your work and happiness, so that your lives will be beneficial for you.

Give daily thanks for all you have. Be good. What does that mean? Be loving, friendly, gracious, charitable, kind hearted, and helpful to all, be God-like.

The Lord your Creator lives forever within you. If you listened to God with your heart and mind, and paid attention to the feelings and thoughts given to you by God, then no leader would ever be more righteous, reliable, genuine, or good to all his people, or love them all equally, just as your heavenly father does his children.

You are all his beloved children. He loves and cares for you all equally, not more, not less than your brother or sister. You all have the same love given to you by your Father/Mother God. Accept this. Learn, and do not be jealous of others.

Everyone has to tread the same pathway of learning, given to you all by God. All pathways are leading to the pathways of righteousness and positive moral qualities, to be next to your Great Spirit.

Goodness is the virtue of moral goodness and good qualities as seen by God.

May a blessing be on all God's children who know this and follow their hearts, for love of the Almighty Great Spirit.

THE WAY OF THE LORD THY GOD

What is the way of the Lord thy God? You may ask!

Think in the ways you think God would think. Do, and say, only what you think He would say.

How do you know what He would say or do? You ask again.

God would only think right thoughts, good, kind, charitable thoughts and do right things, helpful, kind and loving things.

How do you know if what you think or do is good? Listen to your inner being, your spirit. Inside all, everyone alive is a spirit, your true self and the spirit of life.

This spirit is the true, virtuous, genuine, honourable part of you that is also part of God. This is the upright, untainted, bright shining light of Christ within you all. Without spirit, your earthly bodies would not exist.

All of you here on earth are able to set aside a few precious moments each day, to be still, to listen to the tiny voice deep within you. It is the voice you mostly chose to ignore. It is the voice that could lead you straight on your pathway home, not stumbling from it, as so many do. No zig-zagging on and off it, not knowing what is really the right way forward.

Listen. Do what your inner being, your true self says. Hold what it tells you in high esteem. You will not go wrong this way.

Try this. Be still when in trouble. Ask your heavenly Father for help. Listen very carefully. An answer will always be given to you. You must have faith, trust in the Lord your God. All will come right for you in time. Learn to be still. Give thanks for all your blessings, we all have so many. Give that precious time to your Maker. Feel his love enfold you with compassion for all you have been through to be nearer him. God will help you on your earthly journey, if only you would take the time to listen to him. You are never alone. Spirit is always by your side.

On earth, parents have the same problem with their little ones. Never do they wish to listen to the elder, wiser soul, who has already learnt the lesson they now go through.

Remember this example. Try, oh try! Be still! Give God a little of that time, this is all that He would ask of you.

May you all go in peace and harmony my friends, learn from this old soul, do not turn a deaf ear, be wise, be still, and listen.

THE BREATH OF LIFE

The breath of life is given to each and every one of you and to all living creatures and plants, by the Great Creator Himself. Breathe in His breath of love. Breathe out His breath of love to all. The more of this love, pure love, directly from your hearts, that can be spread from one to another, the better a place the world will become for all.

People do not seem to realise that thoughts, all thoughts, good and bad, every moment of every minute, of every hour, of every day, are so very important. These thoughts of ours are living things that travel. They are energy from you, and they travel as fast as the thought is given to wherever it is intended. Prayers are thoughts, wonderful, good thoughts that you send to your God. You should see how they travel- by the speed of light! That's how all thoughts of yours go. Beware of what you think of others, for these thoughts will, by the law of the Universe, return to you one day, and just as fast.

Your every thought builds up the future for yourself and everyone around you. Thoughts gather together, positive to positive, negative to negative, to create the atmosphere and surroundings of your lives.

Spirit World sends positive thoughts to you all, hoping you are receptive enough to pick them up, for positive action to be taken by you. This positive action by you will escalate, leading to more positivity in your thoughts, and in the actions of others, thus leading to more positive ways of responding to all that live on your beautiful planet.

Negativity destroys. Negative thoughts create ugliness, fear, terror, anger and darkness around you all. War is the result of negative thoughts collecting together and generating the energy for the dark forces to arise. In conditions of negativity, dark forces thrive, causing terrible suffering upon earth, to all of God's creatures. This was never meant to be. Always think positive.

Find the positive points in situations around you, work on them. Just watch, see how it works. Positivity in your life creates positivity for all, resulting in happiness, love, good health, and peace for all. Remember to send loving, positive thoughts for the dark places of your earth daily. If all would send thoughts of love, then trouble occurring would be overcome. People could live in peace and harmony, just as God had always intended.

If only you could see the energy, the magic that flies out from each of you with every positive thought you give out. Let loving, positive thoughts build your future for you, your children and their children. Try. We know it is not easy but there is always a positive, learning side to look for, just look a little deeper to see the truth.

Come, let us all send out love to the dark places of the world together to give all people a better life to build on, so all will find it easier to give love. It has a knock on effect throughout the world.

Think about this message a little more deeply, and it will become clearer for you all.

BUTTERFLIES

Look at the beautiful butterflies fluttering around you in the summer sun, at their colours and delicate wings.

Remember the eggs laid by last years' butterflies, the little caterpillars that ate all the young, tender leaves, to grow fat then change into a chrysalis. Think what this chrysalis looked like from the outside, stiff and lifeless. Inside, the fat caterpillar rested. A wonderful process of development took place in this secret little world of the caterpillar. Inside, a miracle was taking place. When the winter was done and the spring sun shone, there was movement inside this tiny chrysalis.

In the warm summer sun the tiny case split open to reveal a wonderful sight. A lovely, delicate butterfly emerged into the sunlight, to sit and dry its colourful fragile wings before fluttering from flower to flower. A fat, heavy caterpillar is reborn as a beautiful butterfly.

So it is with mankind for when the earthly body dies, the spirit within is released. It is free! It is light! It has such beautiful freedom to go wherever it wishes, now the heavy mass of the body is gone. Spirit is ready to start a brand new life of experiences.

Remember this please little ones, when you weep for your loved ones you feel you have lost. They continue to live, but in a far more delicate place, of a much higher vibration. Your loved ones may visit you. They are but a thought away from you. Do not grieve for them. Instead, be happy for their newborn freedom.

Just as each day passes into night when the sun sets, and night becomes a new day with the new sunrise, so the cycle of all life continues. All life is eternal. There is no death, but life after life for all.

SERVICE

Whatever job of work you do, do it as well as you are able! Take pride in whatever your work may be. Do not allow yourself to feel put down by others who think that they are better than you or that their work is more important than your work.

No one job is more important than any other. Each is reliant on another's work. On the earth there are many, many jobs, all equally important, and all work is service. Enjoy your work, for it is service to one another and, as such, service to God.

Remember the great Creator worked to create the world and universes for six days, and rested on the seventh. God invites you all to do this in remembrance to the Great Spirit and as a mark of respect for Creation.

Respect seems to be forgotten totally by most of you. All are busy with the rushing and gathering of the material world. The Sabbath, and respect for the Lord thy God, has been pushed right down to the bottom of the list of importance in society. God, your Father/Mother Spirit, has not forgotten any of you. You are all still loved dearly by the Creator whose heart cries for all the sorrow you create around yourselves in the material world through the energy of striving, of worry, anxiety and tension, just to satisfy a desire, need, eagerness to have the same, and perhaps more than others.

Remember, you are on the earth plane for only a moment in your eternal existence. When you shed your earthly bodies you will have no use for any possessions, wealth or property. They are no use to you in spirit. You will experience great emptiness as you realise that you have missed the most important reason for your life on earth.

The reason you are all on earth was chosen by you for the lessons you are able to learn there. Part of the lesson was to be able to overcome the excessive earthly desire to possess and dominate all. The true reason was to find and fan the inner spark of God within yourself so it glows brightly, shining for all to see.

Help each and every one, you meet as best as you are able, this is the way the Lord wishes it to be. Through your jobs, whatever they are, help, be kind, loving, considerate and compassionate to each other. That is the importance of life on earth. Experience everything around you in joy. Then when you leave earth, your spirit and soul will have grown so all can see they are truly illuminated. Satisfaction and contentment will be yours for you did your very best while at earth's school of learning. You will be ready for your well earned rest at home in spirit with all your friends and family that you met while on earth.

Work well while you have this magnificent opportunity to grow nearer to your Father/Mother God. Do not waste your time on purely worldly things that leave you empty or dissatisfied at the end of your time on earth. Work. Give service to all to achieve that great inner peace and calm, which your spirit, your true self, longs for.

HEALING

You can all help to heal one another. There are many kinds of healers on the earth. But what a fantastic gift to be given, to be used as an instrument for the healing of others by spirit!

Many are chosen to be healers, people full of compassion for others around them. They are willing to give their time and their love to help another. Some give a lot of time for the laying on of hands, so the spirit healers can flow through them and give great peace and comfort for those who seek help in this way.

Unfortunately, some do not understand their gift and wonder why some who come for help still pass to spirit! Why they do not cure all they touch? They become disheartened.

Do not despair. Healing always works, but not always in ways for you to see. Love given is never wasted. Great healing goes straight to the inner being, the soul. It is so important for the soul to be healed. If it is God's will, then the physical body may be made whole and healthy.

To heal is not by touch alone, it is by caring wholeheartedly for others, to listen to people who are troubled, to talk to them, to console them. Give them your time, give them your love, give love to all, or perhaps just a helping hand at times of need.

People do not give time to each other, or listen really carefully to the problems of another as they should. The mind also needs this type of healing. The release it feels after the burden it held is shared or lifted, is tremendous.

People are so involved with self, with all their own needs. Self has become so important, above the needs of all others around them. Do not let the selfishness of self rule you, there are truly inner rewards awaiting all who have compassion for others, and give of their time. Give that time to one another, to help each other. Do not be disappointed if what you do or say to heal another seems to fail. Fail it will not. You will have helped heal what was meant to be healed, and will have given great comfort to the person while being there for them, however short a time it was.

Healing is a God given gift to all, and must never be doubted. Just give time, love and compassion to all you meet and you will help to heal each other this way.

CHILDHOOD

Childhood should be enjoyed, filled with fun, discovery and learning the teachings of Christ the Lord. His teachings should be taught to all the young ones.

These teachings of Jesus, the Son of God, are all teachings of goodness of how to overcome evil when faced with it. From these teachings your children will learn all the good deeds they should follow throughout their lives. All God's children can learn through these teachings.

Let children learn to listen to that inner goodness within their heart centres, this is the way to live and love. Let them learn to love their neighbours whatever colour or creed they are, to respect one another; to love the animals, birds, insects, the plants and all living on the land; to love the fish, the sea animals and all in the sea. The wonderful nature that is around you all is for all God's children to enjoy. Learn to appreciate the good things in life, the gifts that Mother/Father God has bestowed to you all.

Teach the young the wonderful stories Christ told. All young people love stories and Christ your Saviour gave them to you to enjoy. Listen, and learn from them. When told to the young, Jesus' stories sow a wonderful seed of goodness into the little hearts of all who listen. These seeds of goodness would grow and grow as the young grow into strong, loving adults.

There would be no crime or horror on the earth as there is now if they learnt Christ's teaching, always to turn the other cheek. It is much braver to find another way to solve problems than to fight one another and destroy each other.

Christ loves the little ones, and wants them all to learn from his parables, his teachings of love, kindness, compassion for one another. All God's children benefit from the short stories that use familiar events to illustrate situations in daily life, for in each one is a lesson to be learnt from.

All God's creatures, large or small, and all plants need the love of man to be able to thrive alongside man as intended. Think of all this that I have spoken about when you have little ones around you and in your safe keeping. Give them the time and love they need. The foundations of learning through Christ's parables means they will enjoy listening to stories and often will ask for them again and again.

Teach the young to show their love to all God's creatures and to care lovingly for his plant kingdom. Live and demonstrate ways of loving and caring for each other.

What a wonderful world it would be if all would just do these simple things for the little ones. They would grow strong, full of caring compassion for all around them.

Try to bring forth the inner spirit of these children so their goodness shines forth for all to see. Teach them that the faults they see in others are a reflection of themselves so that they can learn from each other.

NATURE'S ELEMENTS

The elements of nature such as wind, rain and sun have great power to give or take the lives of all around them. They alone have the power to destroy mankind. All these elements work in conjunction with the elementals and nature spirits, and should be held in great respect by all.

God rules all of nature, and the elements and nature spirits live by His laws also. They know God's laws and Christ's teaching and suffering on earth for all mankind.

The elements have such a great power within them and man could learn to harness this power, so all can benefit from them. Earth would then be saved from man's destructive tendencies. Man would have no need to destroy trees or dig up earth and sea. As the world is being destroyed all around you, all God's creatures suffer, and will continue to suffer, including mankind.

The elements are there all the time. Knowledge of how to harness their power has been given to mankind by spirit. Spirit is waiting for man to see sense, to use this knowledge before it is too late. The beauty of the earth, your Garden of Eden, is being destroyed all around you. Disease is increasing because your planet is out of balance, which creates disorder throughout your planet. Disorders of this kind bring affliction, and blight to all living things, throwing everything further out of balance. For life as you know it, to continue, you must listen to those who have received instructions of how to power the land, without the earth damage that is reaching havoc proportions all over the world. Nature is out of balance, Mother Earth is in confusion, and is also causing destruction, trying to correct the desolation caused by mankind.

All must listen to those with the knowledge. Follow their instructions of how to harness all the natural power around without the carnage to nature, throwing all into chaos. Act now before it is too late to repair the damage done to your earth. All must always live in harmony, caring for all God has given.

WORDS

Humans use words to communicate with one another. Words are so powerful. You do not realise that each word spoken or thought is living energy. Their sound and intention can cause utter destruction or empowerment wherever they are directed.

Words should thus be very carefully chosen, thought about, before rushing into a statement directed at someone or something. Carelessly spoken words can cause such terrible upsets and pain. Words, your language, can convey precise or ambiguous meanings or messages to another, sometimes causing misunderstanding or annoyance or causing arguments to arise. Then this can trigger the use of blasphemy, turning the air 'blue' with the foul, hurtful, aggressive language. Careless words are often so very hurtful. Often they really are never intended to maim the way they end up doing.

So use language lovingly, caringly, as used in poems, songs, and by lovers. Swallow any ugly words, holding them in your heart. Replace them each time with two or three meaningful words expressing a caring, peaceful intention.

Often people do not bother to pick up their pens to write a few words in a message to friends or family further away from them. This little gesture would mean so much to someone, to know they are not forgotten and are still valued as a fellow friend.

Children learn from adults all the different ways of communication that you use to one another. They will copy you. Be therefore very careful what you teach your young people. They are so easily led into thinking that swearing or shouting is the right way to talk to someone. Teach them correct, caring conversation. Teach ways of expressing themselves in meaningful language that is capable of expressing what they wish to put across to the other, without resorting to the curses used by so many now. The young need to be taught to speak respectfully to another. There are such awful words used from one to another now, that it really isn't a surprise when one of those frequent fights break out. Words can lead to wars, so often they really do this.

Communication is a sensitive way of expressing your views to another. Each of you is equally entitled to your views and your views should be listened to and respected.

However you think, your thoughts are just unspoken words. However you speak of another it is so important to live peacefully in harmony, as God intended. All thoughts and words travel to the people or person intended. These words and thoughts have a habit of returning to the one who gave them out. Be warned of this. Everything you give out returns to yourselves, this is one of the laws of the universe. Therefore use kind speech and kind thoughts to all fellow humans. You are all here to learn from one another. The kinder, more thoughtful you are to each other, the easier it will be for you all to progress into the light.

It is not easy trying to keep using right thoughts and words. Ask daily for help to learn to think, speak, and act as God would. You may be surprised how easy it will be for you.

TRUTH

You all know the great truths the Lord your God gave to Moses to be passed on to all mankind, and through the centuries to all of you.

How many of you listen to your heart, when you know you have not followed these valid truths, and adjust, so as to make your life a life of truth, conforming to a required standard of Divine law. Know them you do, but do many of you live by them? No.

Do you recognise those truths given to Moses? You do, you recognise them all as truth, as the Commandments of God. They are the most important foundations for moulding a man's life. Children, why, why do you not learn? Over and over again the same souls trudge the earth plane, not learning from past mistakes.

Children, try a little harder and be lightened in your load. Then my children, you too will progress up the spheres of life and into the glorious spirit worlds, where you will reap all the good you have learnt and wonder why, oh why, has it taken me so long?

Keep to the simple truths given to man. They are not false, or fictional. Be faithful and loyal to the spirit inside you. To God, be dedicated and loyal.

Man always recognises the truth when he hears sincere truth. He feels this truth in his body, in his heart, and in his whole being. Be simply in your truth. Express your truth lovingly.

Do not turn from the Commandments that hold the key for your lives. Turn the key, and enter into the glorious, bright, golden sun and sit by the Father's side in heaven.

ANIMALS

It is of great value to the people on Earth to get on well with the animal kingdom. It is important for animals to adjust to people. All are on their own soul's journey of growth.

The Great Creator has given you the animals to enrich your lives, for all to learn from, to enjoy their beauty and companionship.

Your doctors realise the importance of animal companions in your homes. By giving you their unconditional love, they give you healing and reduce your stress levels. They give all their love to you. They have great faith in you. They offer their love to you in return for love and care. That is all they ask. Yet still people are cruel and abuse this faithfulness and love that they give so freely to all. As your love is given to them, so it is returned ten-fold by the animals. Look into the eyes of your animal companions. See their soul looking back at you. Do not betray them!

Through the ages man and beast have shared the earth, working the environment with many an animal sacrificing their life as food for man. Many times it is such a rewarding partnership for both sides.

You often hear of how a loving, faithful animal companion saves the life of its human friend, also many a human has given up their lives for the sake of their companion who has grown to become one with them through love.

Animals offer the people of the world pure unconditional fidelity and love to all who are kind and gentle with them. They only ask for food and shelter in return. Your lives are so enriched by these love bindings.

Such love is the love that Mother/Father God wishes you all to learn from. Unconditional love, pure unquestioning love to be given to all you meet and to your Creator who has given you His all. God cares for each and every one of you so very deeply. Love is the secret of life. It is the way of the Lord.

Yes, dear ones, patience is needed on all sides, but what bonds love makes! Bonds of steel that none can destroy. Watch those with animal companions. Look at the joy and love they share together.

Remember too, it is known that those who share their love with animal companions deal with physical and mental troubles far better than those who do not. The body is soothed by such love and companionship

Yes is the answer to the questions so many of you ask, 'do animals live eternally?' They will be waiting in spirit, when you arrive there, with their love.

All living things are energy, all energy lives for all infinity. Lean to give pure, unconditional love to all.

FRIENDS

Value your friends and the friendship they give you so freely. Return all kindness from them for true friends are not always easy to find.

As you progress along the spiritual path, people will flock to you, when they see your inner temple light glowing. They may not at first understand when they are drawn to you, like a moth to a light! Soon realisation will tell them why they are drawn to you, for you are someone who can and will help all who ask. Some people you encounter will form a strong bond with you, also learning to strive and serve their fellow man.

People have to be ready in their own soul to follow the Light, therefore some will be with you for a while and then move on. Still you will give these people all the love, comfort and compassion they seek. These people may need your help and guidance far more than your friends of long-standing.

Never judge others around you. You all have your own lessons in life to learn from. Using discernment, you may see the lessons that others are learning or which they still need to learn. Remember that they may be reflecting aspects of yourself that you also need to address and reflect upon. Remember also that you are there to help them find their own way, their own solutions through love and truth, and it will be your constant love and truth that will empower them to move forward. However people behave they are themselves always loveable. It is the behaviour and patterns of behaviour that may need loving reflection for transformation to take place. How people behave can be as much a cry for help from someone who feels unloved, misunderstood or unloveable, as an actual scream of a plea for 'Help!' To be there at the difficult times for each other is the nature of true friendship.

Lessons can seem so very hard for many, but all lessons are given for your soul growth, you are only given what you can truly cope with in this life. Be strong, carry on carrying on my friends, as we all must to reach our seat next to our Great Creator God.

PAIN

When you choose to follow the path of Light, you may well find yourselves tested over and over again. You and the Divine can build spiritual strength, stamina and endurance within yourself this way. It is as though you are a spiritual athlete in training. Thus you become a strong person whom all can call upon. If you never had any of life's challenges, how could you grow or help those who are in such situations? Your strengths grow as your responses to troubles in your life develop greater love.

The path of Light and growth is not an easy path. It will take you out of your comfort zone! You will be tempted sometimes to take an apparently easier or more glamorous option, to see if you can be drawn from the path of Light. All followers of the Light find temptations are laid in their pathway, to test their faith, trust and beliefs. Keep faith my friends, in God your Creator, whenever such trials come along. God has his hands on your shoulders, to guide you in your times of great need. He will never desert any of his children, whatever they have done. He will always be there for you, helping you recognise weakness or need for change, showing you ways to do this. So take heart, give love, compassion and tolerance to yourself and all you meet.

Pain can indicate a need for cleansing through your physical, emotional and mental energies, so that the light of your spirit may shine forth for all to see. How you interact with pain in your life is very important for your development. Pain is not an aspect of your true self, you are not pain, and pain is not who or what you are. Many of you are troubled by physical, emotional or mental anguish. They can feel woven together in the fabric of your being, so woven that they are entangled. Explore any emotional connections around your experience of pain. For example, pain may often generate fear, increasing the distress caused by the pain. Pain is not eternal- it will pass, as all things on Earth will pass. Hold all in love and kindliness. Focusing on pain reinforces all ties to the pain.

When you offer help and support to those in pain, remember that everyone has within them the key to dealing with their own pain. As you listen, hold your intention to assist others to find their own solution. It may be their opportunity to learn and grow. Be ready to recognise, repeat or describe clues from their own behaviour or words.

Any pain or sorrow you feel when loved ones pass over to spirit is about you not them. You know that your loved ones are now in a place of infinite love and wisdom. Your feelings are about you, rather than expressing unconditional love for loved ones.

There will be no judgement made against you, no one on earth is perfect, just try your best, that is all God asks of you. You all chose to come to earth to learn. You only gave yourself the life and lessons that you knew you could cope with. All will be revealed when you return home to spirit. Then, and only then will you see how well you learnt the lessons of your life on God's earth. You are never alone. Those in spirit guide you daily. Trust in your loving Father/Mother God. Remember you will never be judged. This you humans do to yourselves.

CONTROL

Control is a key to all life while you are on the earth plane. You all control your own lives and the world around you by every thought and sound you make. Negative elements are drawn to you by negative thoughts and speech, and a depressed state of mind is soon yours. Control your thoughts. Think and speak positively, so as to draw the positive elements into your aura, making you a much happier person.

Thoughts and words are all energy. They have their own life force. They never die. Positive and negative energy rotates your planet continuously. The more positive you can be about the world and all troubled situations, the better place it will become. If you always expect the worst then negativity gathers together, gaining strength, affecting all who dwell on Earth.

The same situations occur around you in your own personal lives. Be positive. The universe gives you what you expect. Negative thoughts, speech and actions will only turn your world sour. Positive is what you must be in all you think and do. This will bring Light and happiness into your lives. You all have so much to be happy and joyous about. Each one of you has your own blessings, given to you by the Great Creator. Enjoy your gifts, that is why you have been given them. Your lives on Earth have been given to you to learn from. Enjoyment is meant to be part of that. The Earth was never meant to bring you sorrow.

Look at a pane of clear glass, how it sparkles, shines, reflects, how clear it is. See how you can view the other side so clearly. You all expect to see through a clear window. When you first tune into the spirit world, you don't seem to expect to see very much, just like looking into a frosted window. Next time you tune into the higher spiritual vibrations of Spirit, imagine the clear, clean, sparkling glass you can so easily see through, you will be surprised at what you can see!

What you expect and what you think is what you receive. What you think you can accomplish has an effect on all you do. Expect the best from yourselves, give your best to all then you will receive the best. That is how God's universe operates. It is a Universal Law of Attraction. It is up to all of you to be positive in all you think and do, control your thoughts, speech and actions into a positive way of living.

Learn from your mistakes now! Look around you at the sorrow created by bad, wrong, negative thoughts across the world. Send out your prayers daily to every corner of the world, send out love to all. Think positive, send out good thoughts daily, of how the world will be when all radiate the 'Christ of Light' from within.

The light of Christ is pure and powerful. It can overcome all darkness. Focus beyond the difficulties and challenges, to the promise of the power of Love. Christ focused beyond the crucifixion to the truth, love and strength of His resurrection. Just focus on the power of love and compassion in your daily life and positive life experiences will surround all of you. How soon this will happen is up to you. You can make the difference!

WORLDS

Most of you upon the earth plane think there is only one inhabited planet, just one world, your own world. Those of you who know of spirit, and have contact with loved ones who have passed on, know there is definitely the beautiful world of spirit, with its marvellous clear, bright colours which many with clairvoyant vision have witnessed for themselves.

'There are two worlds then?' You ask. While on earth you are totally unaware of other worlds. You hear of unidentified aircraft, but disbelieve it all. There are so many worlds, each one different from another. Some are very dense, heavier than the earth plane. Many, many worlds are on a very fine vibration, much finer than earth's vibration. The planets you believe to be uninhabited are in fact also lived on by Spirit, in a totally different body from your own. Your planet is in one universe. God created many, many universes, so many so far away for you to imagine.

No, you on earth are not the only creations of God in this universe. There are many. All are differently dressed in spirit energy, to adapt them for their worlds.

Why should you imagine yourselves to be the only creations on earth? Spirit develops in many different worlds, many of you, too, have been on different planets, living in different worlds. When you return home to spirit you will remember all your past existences, wherever they have been. You will also know of the worlds within your own world and also around it, as many existences live alongside of you, in different dimensions around you, not interfering with your lives at all. All the worlds God created are complete just as your world is.

We hope this gives you some food for thought. Perhaps it will open some of your closed minds. Perhaps it will assist them to expand with this information we have given you.

LIFE

What is life, what purpose does it have?

Life is within the creation of a living, breathing organism, which has a tiny part of God within it, which we will call the Christ light. Without this part of the God being present, there wouldn't be any life. The tiny part of God is called Spirit, your spirit. Your spirit helps to develop your soul, the part of you that holds the record of your life or lives.

Everyone lives more than once. All have many, many lives. The purpose of your lives on earth is to experience all types of emotions, all types of possible lives, good, bad, rich, poor, and to master all kinds of personality types. This is necessary to your soul so that your spirit learns and progresses by expanding in experiences of knowledge. The central purpose is that your spirit will eventually realise that unconditional love and pure compassion, are the answers to all questions and all levels of progression. As Jesus once said, 'The Meek will inherit the Earth'.

You ask why progression, what for? The meaning of progress is to become more God-like. As we progress we still speak, think, and act out of love and compassion, loving all life, treating all life well and lovingly.

If the reason for this is to grow nearer to God, to become one with God, then our purpose is to be able, after many, many lives to gain perfection and to join your Father/Mother God. This is the purpose of all life on earth. This is what life is about.

God has given the marvellous plants, animals, birds, fish, insects, reptiles, etc. to share the beautiful earth with you. Each form of life progresses with each life they have. Remember nothing that lives ever dies, it just transforms into spirit. Then when the time is right for you, you go into another life of your choosing.

Yes, you choose when you come to the earth plane. Everyone has free choice here and in Spirit. You choose what you will be, what sort of problems, experiences you will have. The complete life is chosen by you, only you. Enjoy yourselves. We always tell you all to enjoy your learning, to growing nearer to perfection. Enjoy all the life forms around you, their individual beauty and splendour, their company.

Live your lives fully, don't waste them. Life is God's gift to you all. God wishes you to be happy and fulfilled while you are on the earth plane.

Have no fear of passing over to spirit. Just follow the Light, to all your friends and relatives that have gone before you, they will greet you. All animal companions will be there to give you their love, just as they did on earth. People are often fearful of the judgement of God when they pass over. Rest assured, there is no judgement by God. You yourself will judge your life and how you lived it. You will compare it with the task you had set yourself before you went to earth. You are your own loving judge and jury, evaluating your learning of your life's lessons, so that your strengths and weaknesses can provide the basis for your next lifetime of learning and growth, wherever that may be.

LIES

Lies, mistruths, what good do they do? You end up telling one lie to cover up another, another and then another, telling layers of untruths.

Why do people tell lies? To cover up a misdeed perhaps, or something they perhaps should have done and haven't done? To hide an aspect of self that is felt to be unloveable? What a waste of energy. It's such a worry in case you are found out, which is often the outcome. Then there is the worry, anguish, and stress of telling the real truth, eventually facing up to people whom you possibly have hurt by doing this. It all leads to quarrels, fights, negativity, all unwanted trouble for you. What is done is done. It cannot be undone so quickly. People get very hurt by lies and untruthful ways.

'Tell the truth.' This is what you often tell your children. Tell the truth, and you will not end up in quite as much trouble. It may be a little uncomfortable to own up at the time, but this is only for a short while, then it is all over, you will have felt so much better for owning up. If you lie, you feel terribly guilty, uncomfortable, living in fear of being found out.

People respect those who are truthful. They trust them, knowing their trust will not be dishonoured. People who constantly lie find no-one will trust them, they will be thought of as sly, deceitful. They really are only fooling themselves most of the time, others soon see through them.

There is no shame in owning up to forgetting to do something, or perhaps not wanting to do it. Everyone has free will, choosing what and when they do, or do not do things. Do things your own way, this is right. But it isn't right to lie. It is being deceitful to yourself as well as to others. You all know deep down inside yourselves that it is so wrong to lie, it always hurts someone around you. Listen to your inner self. If you choose to ignore its wisdom, then all suffer, including yourself.

Be true to yourself and to your fellow humans. Then you will be true to your own spirit, to the Great Spirit, to the Creator as He wishes you to be. Carry the light of truth for all to see.

PREJUDICE

People of the world hold such unreasonable prejudices against each other. Some dislike another person because they are from another country, others because they come from a different background, or a different part of town. Perhaps you think you are better than another because you have a higher paid job, or drive a bigger car? Perhaps people do not speak as you think they should speak? Why should any of this concern you? You are all God's children, each and every one of you. He loves you all equally. You are all the same inside, you are all spirit.

Each one of you has chosen a different pathway, this is all that is different about you, you are all spirit clothed in flesh. You have chosen different pathways, this is so that you can learn what it is like to be different from those around you, and also to experience the oneness of all. How you are treated, what emotions you feel, are all situations for you to learn from. Each time any of you return to the earth of your own free will, you choose a different lifestyle, perhaps a different gender, maybe a different colour skin and a different personality. Every time you will be just as important as the other people around you, as important as anyone else on the earth. It does not matter what job you hold, all work is service to all.

All souls want to experience every emotion, every situation possible on earth. This is so important to your spirit. This is the way your spirit and soul expand.

When you return home to the world of spirit, you look back over your life to see how you coped with all the problems you had been faced with. Each is so very important for the growth of your spirit. Treat all as you wish to be treated yourselves.

Remember you all are exactly the same in the eyes of the Lord your God. Everyone has the same lessons in life to learn, no one is better than anyone else, no matter where they were born, what job they hold or where they live.

You are all spirit. You are all energy and vibration. You are also all part of each other, part of the One. Love all you meet, help all you can. All are part of the Whole, the Great Spirit which created all life.

COMMUNICATION

Why do you find it so hard to understand communication from one world to the next via a person you call a medium?

Spirit uses a medium as an instrument to communicate to people who wish to have proof of life after life, of life after death. When people realise life goes on, and their loved one is well again, living his/her new life in the next world, they find they can let the pain of loss go far more easily. It is important for you all to know life never ends. You will go on and on being born and reborn. This is part of the way your spirit and soul progress upwards towards joining your Creator.

You use electromagnetic waves in your transmissions of speech and music, which are received in a radio. All of you readily accept radio. You also enjoy the way electrical signals are sent via the airways, into a device you call a television set. This device is designed to receive and convert incoming electrical signals into a series of visible images with sound onto distant screens.

The telephone is another way of telecommunication. It is a way people can and do communicate with each other sometimes across large distances and sometimes involving satellite transmissions. An ordinary telephone involves mechanisms in the brain that cannot be understood yet in your scientific laws.

Some mediums have the clear sense of hearing, (clairaudience), or the clear sense of seeing, (clairvoyance), or clairsentience, the clear sense of feeling energy or presence, or all three.

You are all electrical, energy beings yourselves. Some people have a more open mind and, as such, are able to receive the communication from the spirit world. All of you have the means to develop the power of perceiving sound and visions beyond the natural range of sense. You only have to open your hearts to let the love flow naturally to all, then open up your minds. Tune in through prayer to your Creator. You too could communicate with your loved ones in spirit.

We hope we have explained the way mediums are used as instruments of communication, and given you good for thought. Mediums are ordinary people.

PRAYER

How many of you pray? Do you pray for yourselves, or for the world, and the situations around it at the present time? All the suffering in your world was not intended by your Creator, this needs a lot of prayer.

To pray to your Maker needs your absolute belief in your Lord. The prayers must flow from your heart. All true prayers from the heart are answered by your Father/Mother God.

Most prayers are spent mainly and wholly praying for yourselves. For the solutions to human problems often brought about by yourselves. This is not what true prayer is about.

We know it is often hard to have strong, unshakeable belief in something without any proof of God, or in his actions and promises. To have that absolute faith, that belief in something beyond your control, to have faith and trust in God, to stick to your convictions, adds dimension of love, peace and happiness to all your lives.

Look at how, through prayer and the laying on of hands, some sceptics become absolute believers in something that is so powerful and that has no scientific explanation.

Pray to God. Be thankful for all the gifts you have, feel the vibrations of gratitude in your heart, express them from your heart.
Pray. Pray for your fellow beings, for all life that is on the earth with you.
Pray. Send your prayer with love to the angels who administer the wishes of the Lord.

Faith in God, in his love and kindness, will be rewarded by a better world. When all are giving their love freely to all as was intended, peace will be yours, and you will all be living in the Garden of Eden once more. The world is a beautiful place, it provides for your every need, just as your Creator had planned. Mankind causes the sadness and the pain through thoughtlessness, 'care'-lessness and greed. When things go a little wrong, you all become so negative in your ways and thoughts. Change this response, do the right thing, be positive in all and give out that love to all. Watch, see the world and all who live in it bloom.

Send out your personal communication to your Father/Mother. This is to be your communication, a form of devotion and love. Speak to God. Let Him know of your thanks and personal fears. Be confident that something will be done in God's own time, that all will be well once more.

Do not ignore the Lord as if He doesn't exist. Think of how you yourselves would feel if your own flesh and blood never acknowledged your lives. How hurtful that is. God is Love. He cares for you all, laughs and crying with you, just like any loving, caring parent does. Speak to the Lord, help him put the love back into men's hearts.

FEAR

The world is full of restlessness and anxiety caused by a dread of various things, like losing one's work, impending danger, (which some feel is around every corner). People are rushing here, there and everywhere, trying to do everything at once, causing terrible tension in your minds and bodies. Because of this awful tension your whole being becomes uneasy and you worry over just about everything.

Living in dread of something is an aspect of negativity. It will draw more negative things towards you. Illnesses, such as depression, are often caused through being worried or tense, because of possible misfortune or change, which you feel you will not be able to cope with. All this feeling of apprehension over something that has not even occurred, is completely wasting your lives and energy.

Be more positive about your lives. Accept what transpires in your daily lives. Enjoy yourselves, relax. Just being more accepting and confident about the future, will make you more relaxed, happy and able to enjoy each day as it comes. Why have misgivings about something that may never happen?

God wishes you all a good, happy life on his beautiful world. All the doubt in your minds is ruining your lives. Step out each morning boldly. Be unafraid of each beautiful morning which has been given to you as a gift by your Father/Mother God.

Have faith. We keep telling you this, have faith. Pass the troubles and worries that you feel on in prayer to your Creator. Our God looks after us all lovingly, only your own misgivings bring you the awful angst you feel. Once you have passed your worries on to God in prayer, leave it with love, knowing that the best outcome for you will be sorted out. This will not happen overnight. But trust God and you will come through all 'thick and thin', as you say.

Live life more slowly. Enjoy your work, home life, hobbies, the world and all it offers you. You are spirit on earth. It is only a very short time before you move on to your next existence. Nothing on earth lasts forever. Only your fears make it seem so. Look upon any problems as a lesson to learn from. Do your best with the situations around you. When you have dealt with the problem, leave it behind you and carry on with your life. What has gone is past and cannot be changed. Look forward, live each day to the full, the future is yours. Enjoy your experiences. Know they are your lessons. This is why you chose to go to earth, to learn and grow in spirit.

The spirit world is always with you, never feel you are alone. You always have spirits around that love and care for you, to comfort and guide you. Take time to relax, ask for help and it will be given.

We hope we have explained things a little for you. Go forward. Be confident that we are supporting you always.

DEATH

When someone on the earth plane dies, a terrible grieving overtakes all who knew the deceased. The awful agony of an aching, breaking of the heart, that one they loved is stripped away from them, sometimes in unfortunate or tragic circumstances. This intense sorrow makes those nearest to the deceased feel destitute. The deprivation felt by all who mourn their friends and loved ones, is a natural human process- they all need this important time to grieve. To grieve is part of the healing process that has to happen, before all can go on with their lives. Such a time is important. There is an absence of the physical presence, from which they feel a sort of dejection, or anger at having been left alone. This time is needed to adjust for all, but there really is no reason to fear the permanent end of all functions of life, as you all seem to!

People have such a terrible fear around death and terrible fear of their own earthly death. The force or principle energy of life is impossible to kill in any way. The energy of spirit is eternal life but in a finer form, a less dense world, the spirit world. The sacred essence of every person, the spirit, lives on, it never dies. Yes, the earthly body dies away. It has done its job for the time the spirit was meant to be on earth. The spirit is in every person's body, it is that tiny part of God within each of you. When you die on earth, it is just a transition to another world. You are on the earth, till your earthly learning is completed. Whatever age the person may be when that has been accomplished, the spirit is called back, with all its newly learnt lessons.

You must have faith in the Lord God, your Creator, who would never separate forever, loved ones, friends. This is only for a moment while you are on earth, until your lessons have been learnt. Then your spirit too will leave the earthly body and be called home. Those in spirit celebrate when one of the loved ones passes over to another world that is just a thought away from you all. Perhaps your loved ones in spirit are a little wiser after reflecting over their past lives on earth? They are truly free spirits. A permanent end is impossible- you just cannot kill off energy. Energy is your spirit and soul. Remember, 'I shall be with you in spirit'- such words of truth!

Take heart, do not feel destitute in the intensity of your grief. Remember your loved ones do not wish you to mourn forever. Live a full life. Do this for yourselves and for your loved ones. Then all can progress with their lives, to be nearer our Father/Mother God as our spirits join the whole, united in oneness. Remember friends, your loved ones are well and free, not far from you. They still think of you, and love you dearly. Spirit watches you, helps you, prays with you and for you all. One day you will be reunited when the time is right with friends, family and loved ones. Be strong, go forward, live and enjoy yourselves.

When the initial hurt has passed, a searching for answers and truth can begin. This can be found through a medium on a platform in a Spiritualist Church, or in a private setting. Spirit may pass a message to you from a loved one. Having learnt the truth, the bereaved may pick up the pieces of their lives to the joy of all, including loved ones who are still watching, caring for them from the spirit world.

We here hope this message is helpful to you all.

CHARITY

Charity is often thought of as the giving of money to the needy. This is not so. To be charitable is to be generous in giving time and love to all. A charitable attitude costs nothing. It is a kind, and forgiving attitude towards others. You do not need to be rich to be charitable. 'Spend' time with the old, sick and lonely, demonstrate your understanding of others while helping them, cook a small meal, help with a little housework, or do some shopping for a neighbour- all these acts are charitable. You do not have to lavish expensive gifts, just be indulgent in giving kindly to those you know who would benefit from a kindly hand.

Turn out your cupboards. Stop hoarding all those things you will never use. Take them to places where they can make use of them. You will gain also far less clutter around your homes. This is yet another way of being charitable.

There are so many ways that you can give help to others, even if it is only a kindly attitude towards people.

Be gracious, considerate, and you too will be on the way to being a charitable, loving person. Remember to give without asking for anything in return, this is true charity.

There is no shame in accepting charity from anyone. People all need a little charity from time to time. Be charitable with one's attitude to others, just as your Creator, your Mother/Father God is with all of you, every second of every day throughout your lives.

HOPE

Faith and hope are closely related in your inner emotions. Both generate a desire and confidence in the possibility of an expectation being fulfilled. If you have faith you have hope. More often than not if you have hope you also have faith. They are both optimistic emotions that come from your inner knowing, from your spirit.

Never give up hope whatever the situation is around you. While you are on the earth, living your earthly lives, you constantly come up against troubles of one sort or another. Some are easier to overcome than others. Remember you have chosen this life and all its problems also. This is, as your inner spirit knows, for your spirit and soul growth. None of the problems you come up against are too much for you to overcome. All the trials you have chosen in this life, be it hard to believe at this present time, you have chosen, because you knew you would be able to triumph over them.

Your spirit, your true self, knows this and tries very hard to keep hope in your hearts and minds continually. When difficulties arise, hope is a positive, heartening, encouraging inner will, to help you to trust and come through the dark tunnel of fear and anxiety, into the light once again.

You are but a moment of your eternal lives in your earthly bodies. These terrible times, worries, hardships that you have, are but a minute second of this time. We here know the suffering you go through at the time. It all seems to go on eternally. Rest assured you will triumph in the end.

All tread pathways of life and learning while on earth. How could your spirit or soul grow nearer the Godhead, if you have no challenges and tests to pass? That is all life is, a school of learning. How you deal with your earthly problems, leads to your spiritual progression in your eternal life.

Keep 'Hope' in your hearts, along with faith in your Creator. Then you will overcome all obstacles thrown at you. This will lead you to be a more understanding person who has learnt well from his journey on earth. You will be proud of all your accomplishments when you return home to the spirit world.

Do not worry. Nobody gets through all life's exams easily. All stumble and appear to fail. Just to keep on keeping on trying is what is asked of you. Do your best. Your Father/Mother God wishes you to be happy, and live your lives as best you are able, in just the same way that you wish the best for your children, and ask them to do their best.

Never lose heart. Keep being positive about your life. Hope will always help you to keep on when the going gets tough. Go forward with love and confidence. Keep looking forward to the good things in life. Hope will encourage and keep you strong.

COMPASSION

Compassion enables you to show a kindly attitude towards people. This is a quality many on Earth do not show towards others. We here in spirit know it is not always easy to love one's fellow men, especially when the person is antagonistic towards others. Yet those people need you more than you know. They need you to pour the light of Christ into their dark, mean lives. People are all so very different. You all have your own lessons to learn from in your lives. Each one of you has a different outlook on life due to the circumstances around you. Please try to remember you are all spirit. All are brothers and sisters and a part of each other, a part of the Great One.

The human quality that is best to bring forward, is that of compassion, an emotion of affection, warmth, fondness, respectfulness and goodwill towards others.

Your attitude towards others is reflected in the attitude of others towards you. What you give out, not necessarily in wealth or any material way, but courteousness and warmth will always be returned to you, by the law of the universe. Be generous, sympathetic and tolerant to all you meet. Your attitude towards others, especially to those suffering, or who are unfortunate in one way or another, is greatly appreciated by all. There are so many on the earth who are physically or mentally depressed, or in a weakened state. They get very disheartened with their lives, if warmth and kindness, which costs nothing, is not received. Show a little tender heartedness to all who are depleted in a low path of their lives. It can be such a downward spiral when you are feeling gloomy, miserable and perhaps even unworthy. The dying, the feeble and frail, need your care, love and understanding. Be compassionate towards all, in all circumstances, even where there is hatred.

You will delight, and feel great warmth in your hearts, at seeing a smile on the faces of people whom you meet in your daily lives. Be humble, unassuming, modest, full of warmth, fondness and understanding to all fellow men and creatures. This is how God intended it to be – a world full of love and light.

Unfortunately there is an awful lot of work for you all to do. The world's people are full of bitterness and hatred of one another in many places, perhaps even within your own homes or neighbourhood. Hostility and ill will is so terribly negative and destroys all so easily. Let the light of Christ shine from you! Go forth to transform the dark areas and it will cost you not a penny. A small price of time, assistance and tolerance of all is asked, and then the light will soon encompass the world.

Remember to give out the love you are so freely given by the Lord your God. Reach out towards all, perhaps even give a cuddle, or a warm embrace, if you are able and feel it would be acceptable. There is healing in the power of touch and it does cheer people up to know they are loved. To give like this, without pretentiousness, without payment is so rewarding. Be forgiving. Provide loving attitudes towards all God's creatures, love and more love, and watch the world change. It is up to each and every one of you to transform the darkness on earth with your compassionate love.

COMPOSURE

Why do so many of you lack confidence in yourselves? You can only do your best in your lives, no more. Be collected in your thoughts, words and actions. Make sure you're being level headed and positive in what you do. Positivity brings more positive things into your life through the Divine Universal Law of Attraction.

When you are nervous, lacking confidence, feel hesitant, insecure and self doubting, stop. Look at what we have told you, just do your best with a positive attitude. Why suffer?

Lots of you admire the people around you who seem totally composed. They have calmness around them, they seem totally relaxed with no earthly worries to trouble them. Would it not be lovely to have such an existence? No, your earth life would be of no use to you. You are in the earth school to learn all about troubles and emotions. No one is without worries of some sort or other, it is just that these people, whom you admire for their composure, stay calm and centred in their truth.

Calmness, especially of the mind, is important to your whole being. For good health, try to stay positive, tranquil and, above all, try to be satisfied with your life. Take a little time to yourselves, even if it is just five or ten minutes. Everyone can spare that. Be relaxed, breath in deeply and breath out slowly, become at ease, become calm. If situations arise to ruffle you, breath, relax, don't get agitated and worried. Show the outside world that you are calm, by using a calm, steady voice. You will be amazed at the difference this makes to the reaction you receive in return.

Always try to keep unflappable or 'cool', as you say. A peaceful, still way to regain control of one's emotions, after a shock or terrible disappointment is to breath calmly and deeply. Show the world this person who is level headed, confident in every situation. Not showing uncontrolled worries or anxiety, but always being positive and showing a certainty, will convince others this is how you are. They will admire your composure, giving you respect. Living this way will calm your mind and body, eventually leading to better overall health. It may be an effort at first, but seeing the results of composure will make it easy for you to continue.

God wants the best for his children. When worries get a little too much for you to handle, offer the problem up to the Lord. He will take care of your problems if asked. It may not be right away, but you can rest assured that when and what the outcome is, will be for the best. Have faith and pray. Be calm, peaceful, placid and gathered together in composure. Your life will change for the better.

MEDITATION

This is an ideal way to wind down and relax body and mind, a way to refresh yourself anytime you can snatch ten minutes to yourself. Once you learn to meditate you will feel the benefits, it lifts the pressure off your body and mind, and is a very good way to improve your overall health.

The natural energies within you flow freely, cleansing and revitalising you, quietening your mind and body. These energies are all very profound. People in the East have known the real value of meditating for centuries. People in the West are just realising the benefits to be gained by just meditating a short time each day.

Unfold your heart-centre by daily meditation. A relaxation meditation will awaken the Christ love within you. You learn to understand that your body really is the temple for your presence on Earth. Learn to respect and honour yourself. This way you attract the Christ-power into your heart, you learn what inner peace and love really mean. People who meditate regularly look forward to the time they've allotted to themselves. Let the Light and love flow into your lives.

There are many ways people meditate. The easiest way to start is to find a quiet place where you will be undisturbed for ten minutes or so. Sit or lie comfortably, as straight as possible. In this way, energies can travel up and down your body freely. If you like you could light a candle so you have a focal point, helping you to clear your mind of daily problems. Another way is to close your eyes and think of a flower, or just daydream. Many of you are rushing about so much that you may even find it a challenge to sit still and meditate. It is also a good way to recover from an illness or operation.

There are many books written on meditating, also music tapes, choose what method you feel most relaxed and comfortable with.

As you progress you will become aware of your own Christ Spirit within yourselves, finding yourselves opening up to inspiration from the Spirit world. Spirit is able to draw close to you while you are still and relaxed. Your own spirit inside your body, which is your true self, will start to expand and connect in new ways with the Divine force of life. You will develop new understandings of why you are on the earth. You will gain insight into the relatedness and connectedness of all life.

We hope you will take time to learn to meditate for all the benefits it will bring to you, including a great inner strength and peace, giving you a positive way of life beneficial to you all.

RELIGION

Religion is always being blamed for a lot of the conflicts in your world. Why is there so much bitterness, disagreement and fighting between people who hold a different faith from one another?

God is visualised differently from country to country, even different Christians have their own personal view of the Almighty Power, God. It does not matter how you imagine God as long as you are a caring person to all God's creations. Have faith in the Divine Power, the supernatural power of God, who has always had control of your human destiny. God has given you all free will and does not control everything that goes on in the world.

God is a loving parent to all living things he has created. Our Creator wants you all to be at peace with one another, to be tolerant of others and their faith. You may not agree with them, but it is not for you to judge another's faith or way of life. Each spirit, when given life in an earthly body, was also given total free will in all things by their Father/Mother God. You have no right to pressurise and inflict your personal views upon another. Each person has the religious belief that is appropriate to them and their way of life at that time.

All the Divine Spirit God asks of each and every one of you is that you live in peace and harmony with each other and all around you. It does not matter what religion another has, or what colour skin their spirit is clothed in, you are all brothers and sisters in the school of learning from one another. All religions lead to the One ever- loving God. There is only One Creator.

All that is asked of each and every one of you is that you live in peace and harmony with each other, treating everything living with the love and respect you expect yourselves. If all of you would follow these words given, then the Christ light would grow, shining out from each of you. You would all be living in the beautiful world God has created for you, with everything to meet all your needs, for all to enjoy together, just as Adam and Eve were first given in the Garden of Eden.

Let peace and understanding start with you, be loving, tolerant of all you meet. Remember you are all part of the Great Spirit yourselves. It is just that you are all experiencing your own needs to grow at this present time. If you love your neighbour, watch how the flame of love catches on to the next, and the next. Let this all start with you.

ADVICE

When you have problems, how many of you listen to friends, family or the Church, giving you advice?

Share your problems, lighten your load, yes, but do not always take the advice of others. They all mean well we know, but realise this: each one of you has unique problems that are unique to you, caused by your surrounding friends and family, and perhaps work. Each person's circumstances are different. Not even a problem which may seem the same is going to be the same. All of you are individual spirits with personalities of your own. The advice others give can only be based on their personal circumstances and however well meant cannot provide the perfect answer to help another on their pathway. The perfect answer lies within you!

Step back from your problem. View it calmly, go deep within yourselves, listen to your heart, to your higher self, the Divine within you. This is where you will find the true answer to all life's problems. Take time to talk to God. Lay your troubles before Him. Ask for His understanding and help. He will never let a child of his down. Listen, feel, and trust in your heart- you will know what to do or say.

Remember you are an individual and individual answers are needed, given by your true self.

HOME

Everyone wants and needs a home. Many unfortunate souls on earth are destitute, feeling completely abandoned by society. These people are so grateful for a shelter from the elements, yet so many of you, with comfortable dwellings, are dissatisfied with what you have. Many of you are always wanting a bigger, better place- better than your family and friends.

This is not what a home is meant to be! It is meant to be a shelter from the elements, however small, a dwelling for loved ones to share. Home is a place where loved ones are comfortable sharing the same space.

A home, what should it be? It need not be a mansion. A mansion can be so cold and unwelcoming if the love is not there. Bigger is not necessarily better.

All the persons living together in one household, one's own flesh and blood, one's nearest and dearest, should all find that their home is their sanctuary from the outside world. This is where flesh and blood stick together through thick and thin, or at least it should be. It does not matter how large or small an abode is, the tiniest place can be made into a loving environment. Home should be where two people can raise their brood of children in love and safety from the outside world.

When you visit friends, relatives or associates, notice the difference in each home you enter. Sometimes it is small and overcrowded, full of love and very welcoming, so comfortable that you do not notice that they have no floor covering, or the latest technology. A home should ooze love to all who enter therein. It should feel familiar, warm and loving. So often it is the informal homey pad, where people are natural, modest, unaffected by what others have or do, that you feel the happiest in.

Your own home is your territory if you like. You are the ones who put the warm and welcoming or cold vibrations into your homes. Which home would you really prefer to visit, the simple everyday domesticated, ordinary house, with laughter and the cosy fireside hearth welcoming you, where you are welcomed to make yourself at home and relax; or a large house filled with expensive items you dare not touch. We here know which dwelling we'd rather enter into.

It is up to all of you to choose which sort of home you'd like to live in and raise your young. We can tell you that the young flourish and develop in a loving environment, rich or poor, far happier than any show house. Their friends can come home and feel totally at ease in a homely, loving place.

We have often mentioned that love makes the world go round, it truly does, as does love make a family home a place all love to return to, at the end of the day. It is your choice how you live, but please pour your love into the ones you hold dear to you, give time, patience, and be tolerant to each other also. All this will make a truly happy home.

FRUITS OF THE SPIRIT

Friends, it is extremely important that while man is living on the earth, he learns to serve. You are on the earth by your own personal choice. You are here to give service to one another, as we have told you many, many times.

Jesus told us all, "You shall love your neighbour as yourself". You have your God-given freedom. But do not use your freedom as an opportunity for self-indulgence. Take great care not to hurt or destroy one another. If you do talk badly about another, by the law of the Universe the same will be done to you. Remember this. Do not hurt one another, with anger, strife, quarrels, envy or jealousy. This is not the way to live by the Spirit.

Help each other to learn about the Spirit so that all can go forward as Christ intended. Offer a helping hand to each other. Use the Fruits of the Spirit whenever you can. These, as you know, are love, truth, peace, joy, patience, kindness, generosity, faithfulness, gentleness, and self control.

There is no place in your lives for hatred, fighting, murder, jealousy. Be pleased for your brothers and sisters when they step forward in life and spiritual progression. Know that as they do this they are helping you also.

Life is full of opportunities for all of you along your chosen pathways. Some of you gladly go along and take these opportunities to give of your best as you travel the way. Others wish to plod along and pass the opportunities by, perhaps not even recognising what progress may lie ahead through such opportunities. Each one of you has a purpose on earth to fulfil. All of you are very different. All of you will fulfil your tasks differently. What is important is that you live by the fruits of the Spirit. These fruits are love, not envy, hatred or jealousy, which is so common among peoples of the earth. Not everyone will be a great success but everyone will accomplish what is meant to be for them, as long as they do their best and give service to all they meet. Be pleased for each other. All of you are working for spiritual advancement. Those of you who are working are spreading the love and truth of spirit in your own way. You are all working as one for the good of the whole.

Keep these words close in your hearts. Many of you forget your spiritual purpose for coming to the earth and have a tendency to negative behaviour. Jealousy and competitiveness have no part to play in service where there can be only love and the great truth that our Master Jesus taught us Himself.

Go forward now brothers and sisters. Help all who wish to walk the path of our Lord God.

SYMPATHY

We here in the Spirit world see all your troubles, woes and fears. We have a great sympathy with you all.

You all tread the pathways you have chosen for yourselves. Take care, listen in your quiet moments to us, we will guide you as best we can.

We here in Spirit have trodden the same roads and byways as yourselves. We came upon the same trials and troubles that befall each of you. We are here, sending you our love, waiting for you to listen, to guide you onwards.

With great understanding we watch over you and guide you as best we are able. For we here are not allowed to interfere with your personal or material choices. We can only help you to gain strength and insight about the choice of roads ahead. The choice is always yours. Our Father/Mother God has given each and everyone of you free will, so you may experience, learn and enjoy the earth life you have.

Never think you are alone. We are always with you. Never have fear, but avoid fear itself, for this will drag you down. This is not what we wish for you. Be positive. Keep your spirits high. Nothing can hurt your true self. Your spirit is eternal and eternally loved by your Father/Mother God.

You are eternally blessed by God as you walk forward on your life's pathways. The pathways you yourselves, have chosen, go ever onwards. Carry Truth and Love within you for others to share and to learn of the Light of Christ which burns within your hearts.

STRESSES AND STRAINS

Brothers and Sisters of the world, many of you are burdened by the stresses and strains of living in your fast and furious world.

Many of you know not how to 'Unravel' as you say. Take a little time to yourselves each day, sit in the quiet. Think of the Lord your God. Breathe in His breath of life and love. Breathe out love and peace to all. Once this has been done a few times, deep relaxation will become yours, the peace, the deep inner peace for which each of you search, will be yours. This peace within you is the life spark of God, in all of you.

Commune daily with this peaceful part of God within you, your daily stresses and strains will become a little easier to bear. You will realise these problems are not that important. Do not fret over little things. Your minds were created for greater things, to open up to the power of the Great Spirit all around you.

Take time and indulge in time with Spirit, your Spirit will feel like it's been given a boost and extra strength to cope with all problems. You will become much more contented and truly uplifted.

GREED AND DISSATISFACTION WITH LIFE

Often people are so inverted, thinking of self continually, instead of giving thought to others. When self is so important, one cannot link into the Great Universal Energy Love, this in turn leads to a disconnection with love, leaving people feeling unloved, rejected, confused and depressed with life.

God sends this free, great unconditional love to all, never leaving anyone out. It is a self-disconnection to Love that causes so much pain and suffering. Selfish self-centred ways of life only lead to trying to control others' lives, not accepting life as the great joyous freedom, to expand your true spirit within all of you, the God Spirit.

Dissatisfaction with life leads to greed, self-indulgence, no long term happiness, and problems with their personal relationships. These people do not know how to love themselves. Learn to be loving. Feel the love from within for all, including yourselves. Give love freely to all, even to people you may think of as enemies, all need this love life force. Love is totally free and should flow continually from one to another. It is not for one person to hold on to for self, if you do not give love, how can you possibly expect love and compassion in return from others.

Look for that love light in all, whoever they are. Watch, listen, feel the difference in your personal lives. Learn to give generously of self. This is the true way. Life should be lived in harmony, service to one another, regardless of what another gives to you.

People must learn to live in communities of sharing and giving, not the self-gratification so many continually seek. These people miss out on so very much in life. Being able to give of self, to share all things, leads to such great rewards. Be humble, generous, giving. Leave that ego, the greedy, defensive, arrogant, proud part of your lower self behind you. Experience the deep love you have within you all.

Relationships will flourish when you are an open, loving person. Be positive, praising your fellow man. Find fault in others, and they in turn will find fault with you. Leave bitterness, resentment and greed which are so destructive, behind. Build yourselves a better future, a far better life.

Communicating lovingly, honestly, leads to contentment. All will have some disappointments, frustrations in life, and no one is perfect. Leave the hurt behind. Do not let it fester within. If you are more responsive to each other's needs, ignoring the imperfections which you all have, life will be much more enjoyable for all.

LIVES

Why do you fear death so? It is just one state of being exchanged for the next state of being, in your external lives. It is a time when the heavy material body is cast aside, as a new part of you takes you to the next part of your existence as a lighter, free body.

It is a time for all to rejoice. A new life cycle is a new beginning, a chance to look over things that went on in your earthly life. It is a time to reflect and ponder as to how it perhaps should, or could have worked if you'd taken a more loving, giving pathway.

Your lives are for living, experiencing as much as possible at the same time as helping your fellow man as and when you are able. The emotions experienced in the earthly body cannot be experienced in any other place. This is why, while you are in Spirit, you queue to revisit the earth plane. It holds so very many variations of life for you to savour and learn from. Learn well friends. Enjoy each new emotion and each situation that you encounter on your journeys.

Each experience has great potential value according to the way you deal with it. When you return home to the world of Spirit, you will see just how well you accomplished what you went to earth to learn.

On passing over to the spirit world you can marvel at all that went on around you, all of which you were so unaware of at that time. The help you had from all your spirit friends and family, the angels and nature spirits, not to forget the elements. It is a time to take stock, and to consider carefully the rights and wrongs that took place. Next time you will try to put right any mistakes. This way you will carry onwards, towards the ultimate goal, through many more stages of learning, towards that goal of sitting next to our Father/Mother, in the glorious light of Goodness.

Remember dear friends, death is just a transition from one life to another form of Being. There is no death, just a continuing school of learning and resting, till all has been experienced and that ultimate Goal is reached.

Enjoy your lives, friends and all the learning. In every experience you encounter, thank God for the privilege of the learning it has brought you. Thank the mighty Creator each day for all you have, each and every day of your lives.

GIFT FROM GOD

One of the greatest gifts God has given you all is unconditional love. This unconditional love is within each of you, deep within your spirit. It is there for you to uncover and to share with all God's creations.

Look at your fellow men and women. See their inner goodness, the Christ Light. Each time you meet a person look past the earthly person with their imperfections. They are on their pathway of learning just as you are.

To share unconditional love with all equally, is to ignore all the wrong they may do, the selfishness they may show, even the cruelty they may dish out to others. You need not like what you see or the person, but we ask you to look further, to love the Spirit within, which is part of you, part of the 'Whole'. We ask you to love, to guide and not to condemn. They are fellow spirits in their earthly clothing, on their individual pathway of learning and progression, a pathway you do not understand. It is not for your understanding.

All you need to understand is that each and every one of you have the same pathways of learning to walk, some learning lies behind you in a past life, other learning lies ahead for you to experience.

Do not condemn others, lest they condemn you. Love all you meet, we know this is hard for you to understand with your earthly minds. It is necessary for all to love and cherish all life, and to help each other along your chosen pathways of learning. Teach each other the correct way to live the way your brother Jesus taught you, the way of Unconditional Love for all, and of forgiveness for all their mistakes, as we all make so many.

FORGIVENESS

There is not anyone who has lived on the earth who did not make mistakes or trespass against another. It is human to make mistakes. This is the way you learn, through working through your mistakes. Be merciful and forgive another when they have made mistakes. No one should condemn another, nor should they blame themselves for the mistakes they make along their pathway. Forgive yourselves, do not hate yourself. Admit the wrong. Then carry on with your life and learn from the mistake. Always admit to a mistake, others will look up to you for being so open and honest. Admire the honesty in others who have the courage to own up to their failings.

To be able to forgive is not of the earth, but a gift from God as it is of the spirit to be forgiving. You must be able to excuse another's mistakes, to give absolution, to be merciful to another. To forgive is to cease all blaming, to grant a pardon, however large or small the mistake is. Do this. Free the person from a penalty or from obligation to you. This must be done from the heart and you must truly mean 'I forgive you'.

No one is perfect on the earth. You are all learning different lessons. Trial and error are part and parcel of living as a human. Jesus said in his teachings that there is no trespass that cannot be forgiven. He forgave everyone all their mistakes and loved them no less for making mistakes.

You are in the university of life, and in order to learn, mistakes will always be made. Do not feel inadequate because of your mistakes. Forgive yourselves as you forgive others. Always forgive with love and kindness. Be compassionate to each other. Do not let an error divide your love or respect for one another.

You must be able to accept apologies gracefully, to bear no malice. Let bygones be bygones and just carry on with life as if nothing happened. Make the most of your life on earth. Learn all you are able while you are there. It is but a short time and there is so much for you to learn about each other.

EGO OF MAN

Every person has an ego. The ego tries to take over your life at every opportunity. Be aware and guard against ego winning through. Ego has only concern for its own interests and welfare. It is an obsessive love for self. Ego makes a person very self-centred, with an inflated sense of self importance, drawing all possible attention to itself and wanting continual appraisal. This self-absorption and self-centredness makes it difficult to be aware of others and their needs and is totally against all of God's teachings. A person whose ego has taken over is conceited, a boaster, full of him/her self, with little or no time for others as they think they are a step above all others. Remember you are all equal, no-one is better than another. Ego leads to a lack of love for their fellow man, and all that self gains is narcissism.

All the teachings of Jesus are of love for one another and for self, but not in the self-centred way of Ego. Unconditional love does not exist where there is ego, for this rules a person.

Jesus taught us never to seek the limelight, but if it comes, to stand in it with humility and love for all around. Push ego aside, love one another. Be pleased for another's progress in life. Never envy, yearn or be jealous. Aim to be a loving friend to everyone. Support others as much as possible. Until ego is pushed aside, real love will not be felt for self or for others. Ego has no place in the life of a spiritual person. Aim to have clarity in all cases, with little or no time for others as they think they are a step above all others. Remember you are all equal. No-one is better than another. Some are further along the path, but that only means that they offer help to others so they can travel along together.

Until ego is pushed aside, real love will not be felt for self or for others. Ego has no place in the life of a spiritual person. Aim to have clarity in all cases you come across. Concern yourself only with what is relevant. Co-operate with others lovingly. Be driven yes, but by love, nothing but pure love. Love is the pure impulse to give of self to share with others, to help one another whenever and wherever possible. Care about everything around, yet be attached to nothing, this way you keep greed at bay. Be gentle with all you meet. This is the quality of a person with good thoughts, a person who will listen and do their best to help everyone. Be happy. Do not strive for too much. Know how lucky you are to be alive. Be exhilarated with your life and what you are learning. Keep your spirits high, be joyous. Above all be content, satisfied with life as it is. Be willing to change, to accept circumstances which arise, deal with these circumstances, restraining all selfish desires.

Ego has no place in your lives, always push it back down. Walk away from it, let it go. Never let it raise its ugly head in ways that control you.

FAITH

What is faith? Faith is something you feel deep within your very being. It is the foundation of life, a corner stone, perhaps, to build upon, making it possible to know God better.

It does not matter what specific system of religious beliefs you have, just that you have a complete trust in your God, His actions, His plans for you. This is faith.

To have faith is to have such a strong, unshakeable belief, even without material proof, to have complete confidence and trust in the Creator of all. When a person has this complete faith, it does not matter what religion it is as long as they truly believe in God. There is but one God, so whether you are Catholic, Buddhist, or Jehovah Witness, it does not matter as all paths lead to the one Great Creator God. It is important that you have a belief, and faith is the assurance that you can rely on, no matter what happens in your life. You need the confidence in the complete loyalty of God and His love for you. All of you are special to God, you are all His children, He loves each one of you equally.

Honour your God, be sincere and devoted. Stand staunchly by your beliefs. When troubles come your way do not doubt that God is by your side. He will never let you down. Believe brethren. Remain true. You will see that all has been carefully planned for your life. All will come right for you as it was planned so long ago, before you came to the earth.

Be enthusiastic about your life, often the goals are high, but you know you can reach them, that all the help you may need will be given to you, freely and lovingly, by God. Keep your eyes on the target ahead. Do not get distracted from your goal. Have courage. Be sure your aim is right, then ask God for help. Keep your dignity no matter what happens in your life. You are special, trust God, just keep putting one foot in front of the other one step at a time. Stay positive about your life, faith is the key to all life. Things will work out as planned, just be content. This is a quality of a wise person, whose faithfulness to God is unswerving to the end.

Understand friends, that every event in life is beneficial to you.

SELF LOVE

Every one of you is Spirit first, human second. All of you are very special and greatly loved by God. Realise this and you will find a new inner strength. God loves you all deeply, no matter what you do or say, you are special to Him.

Jesus once said, 'Love your neighbour as yourself'. This is very important for you to do, but first you must learn to love yourself, or you will not be able to love others. Once you have learned to love yourselves as God loves you, the world will seem to change for you. All love softens hardness, it makes all things possible, it turns trauma into a lesson for you to learn from. Things change for the better where there is love. Allow yourself to love all, this is so much easier once you can love yourself, and realise there is a deep peace inside you. This is your part of the 'Whole', a part of God, you are an invaluable spirit, and your life and the way you personally live it are also unique and invaluable.

Keep all your thoughts simple, and based on love. Keep moving forward in life. We realise it can be hard for you to love yourself, but when you are able to, you will be able to feel the sweetness of life, of personal knowledge. Love will shine out from your eyes for all to see. Love will always return to you. Accept everyone as they are, look past their flaws and love the real inner person.

When you can love freely, you will be tolerant and recognise the beauty and individual uniqueness of everyone on earth. To love everyone, you will find a newfound freedom. Be completely absorbed in love for your God and you will always be protected.

A LESSON FOR ALL

The trials and tribulations of life are your lessons in life for gaining insight into emotions like despair, greed, desires, contentment, happiness, etc. These emotions are of great value to your inner being, your spirit. It is through such emotions and their lessons that your spirit can progress nearer to the ultimate goal that you all wish to attain, a Oneness with God.

Step forward each morning into the day with a thankful enthusiasm, knowing all you do, say and feel, are to your advantage. Be caring and loving to all you meet. Treat them as you too wish to be treated. This is the way you can be sure of giving your best. Always think before you utter a sound, remember words and thoughts have lives of their own and can do untold damage to another. Think of Jesus, of how He walked his pathway through life. Make it your goal in life to think, speak, and act as He did. Jesus came to show the way, many still have not learnt. When all follow His example, the world will be such a wonderful place to be. Even Mother Earth responds to your actions and emotions, she always reflects the feelings of her inhabitants. If the world is violent and angry so is she.

DETERMINATION

Many on the earth today lack the determination in their earthly lives, to carry on believing in their faith, to enable them to get through their lives with dignity.

Remember to have and to keep your faith in your God strong. Be enthusiastic about your lives. Determination is the energy you need to keep going against any obstacles put on your pathways. We realise that at times, when you lack the determination, the odds seem to be stacked against you. This, your Father/Mother God, would not allow. You are never given any more than you are able to cope with. You are all much stronger than you give yourselves credit for.

Keep your head high. Keep your dignity, faith and courage as you focus on your personal goal in life.

Your life is like a multi-faceted gemstone. As you go forward against each test that you come across, each facet is shining. When you return home to the world of spirit you will know how well you learned your lessons, by the way your gemstone facets have been polished.

Keep the determination that each of you were given at the start of your earthly life and stride forward courageously.

WINDOWS OF THE SOUL

Look into the eyes of the newly born baby. See the wisdom, the knowledge within the eyes of the little one. The eyes are the windows of the soul, as many of you often quote.

Take good care of your young ones. They know so much, and hold a lot of wisdom for the world's future.

There are no new souls now on the earth. All souls in incarnation have been many times before. Each one is at a different level of spirit evolution.

Cherish the little ones, give them your love. Teach them how to live in the world today. Show them how to live in the world. Watch them grow and see the gifts they have brought with them. It is up to you, the adults, to nurture the spiritual side of the young so they may awaken and show their gifts for mankind to share.

LIFE IS BUT A DREAM

Your life is but a dream my friends, everything appears to be real. It is real to each one of you now as you are acting the play you came to participate in. You are all like actors upon a stage, playing out the roles you chose to play. You are portraying the characters and personalities you have chosen. You are living through all the emotions towards the other players in the play. You are all, we repeat, all just playing a role part for a very short time to gain the life experiences your soul felt you needed this time around. But this is not reality. This is illusion. This will pass. Reality is eternal.

Reality will be yours again, once you return home and are with your spirit family and friends. You will then judge yourselves as to how well you felt you played your part in the Life Play you had just completed. Then, just like an actor, you will rest a while before you decide which part in which play you will choose to portray next.

Enjoy your dream. It is your dream to live and enjoy. As you live your part you will learn all you came to learn. Next time the play may be easier or harder, depending on how you personally view the way you performed this time round. This happens to all of you until you have played every part you can possibly imagine, and some you may never have thought of.

Bless you, dear friends. Do not judge yourselves too harshly, we all make mistakes. This is how we too learn. You can only do what you feel in your heart is right at the moment.

THE POWER OF THOUGHT

Friends, we here in the spirit world wish you would be very careful about what you think. Your very thoughts are so important, why have you not realised this?

Mother Earth responds to your innermost thoughts, whether they are of the positive nature or the destructive or hopeless negative thoughts so many of you put out, especially in times of trouble. We here understand that you find it hard to imagine that your thoughts form your world tomorrow. Spirit always wishes to help you. Please listen to us. It is so important that you all keep positive and loving to all God has created. It is a big responsibility that everyone has for their thoughts.

Please try to be optimistic about the future. There has always been a certain amount of trouble flaring up around the world. Send out your powerful, positive thoughts. Do not stop because you feel it is not working. We here can assure you all that thoughts go where they are intended to go. Eventually, if you all persist, then the world will become a place of peace, where all live in harmony with one another. We have spoken of this before, just as we mentioned before that thoughts travel just like your prayers. You are all far more powerful than you realise, do not doubt yourselves as you so often do, God gives you the power to mould the world as you wish it to be. Speak with love, help others awaken to the truth of God when they are ready to listen.

The world has been here far longer than your scientists would have you believe. It has always survived the vast destructive forces that have engulfed it throughout the ages. Your world will survive, but it is up to you how the future transpires. Your world is very important for the progression and development of the spirit world, as most of you have already learned. Help each others to understand. Learn and awaken to the unconditional love that all have within themselves. Give love to one another, to make your world a better place for tomorrow, and all the tomorrows to come. Hard as it may be to believe, the world today is as you all have made it.

WILL GOD FORGIVE ME?

Many of you ask, 'Will God forgive me my sins?' We will answer you as simply as possible.

No, God does not forgive, as forgiveness is an earthly thing to do. It is impossible for our God to forgive us, as God never passes any judgement on us. He only loves us. This is the total unconditional love, where this is given in total truth, it is impossible to forgive or lay any blame. Your strengths, mistakes and weaknesses are known and you are unconditionally loved. You will not be judged by God. You will be assisted to learn and grow.

You my friends, must learn to forgive in such a way also. When you forgive a person who has injured you in a terrible way, you will also eventually forget the hurt, as it grows dimmer in your mind, as time goes on. To forgive a person totally, from the heart, is also to forget the pain as the two are linked together, it is impossible to truly forgive another without also forgetting the hurt.

When you have learned to forgive someone you will benefit, as you will be released from the 'Karma' you had made for yourself and, as such, you will be able to progress in your spiritual life. To be in harmony with God you have to be able to forgive with God's love. God will help all who sincerely try to do this, as it is 'His will'.

You will also have helped the person whom you have forgiven, as you have 'let them off the hook' as you say. This will lessen their personal 'karma', as they will not have to wait until they are in Spirit to try and seek your forgiveness. This way they may consciously feel remorse in the world of Spirit when they pass over and be freed from the 'karma' they would have had to suffer by the lack of forgiveness from those on the earth.

We hope we have helped you understand the full importance of forgiveness as God would, from the heart, it is very important for you to put right any hurt while you are able to, before you reach the spirit world.

MATERIAL AND SPIRITUAL WEALTH

Do you remember Jesus talking to a young man and telling him to sell his worldly possessions and follow Him, then saying, "It is easier for a camel to go through the eye of a needle than for someone who is rich to enter the Kingdom of God." Do you understand the meaning of this simile? Many of you do not, so we will explain it to you in today's language. You all know that when you pass over you are unable to take any of your worldly possessions with you. They are of no importance in the realms of the Spirit. Wealth on the earth should be equally shared among you all. God does not tolerate greed in an individual. There is nothing wrong in being rich in the material sense, as long as the person is still humble, willing to serve all others materially and emotionally with love, joy and giving generously of self. It is important not to feel it is a duty to give, but to be generous from the heart, realising that you are no different from anyone else, rich or poor. You need to be compassionate to all and to be sensitive to all, whoever they are.

Perhaps you are not rich in the material sense, but are gifted spiritually? Then it is still extremely important that you too remain humble, happy, compassionate, joyful and sensitive to those around you. You must never feel any resentment towards others whom you feel may be better off, materially or spiritually. All God's gifts are of equal value, we have told you all this many times. They are also all of equal importance. It is important that you help all God's creations equally lovingly and with an open heart. Each person in the world has at least one gift that God has entrusted them with, whether this is material or spiritual, it is of equal value. Offer it widely to others. All gifts are not yours alone, they are for everyone you know and meet. Never be self-indulgent, trying to keep your gifts for yourself alone. Share them around and learn from the sharing. Those who give freely of their gifts learn many emotions, see many situations around them, enabling them to progress as God intended them to spiritually. Awaken to the real purpose of your being here on earth, the real purpose of your lives.

Remember friends, the simile of the rich man. If you clutch these gifts of the world to yourself, then you have kept what was meant to be shared and 'will not enter the Kingdom of God' as Jesus said. Do not make this mistake and then suffer the terrible anguish of what could have been when you reflect on your life in the world of Spirit.

INNER STRENGTH

Friends, do you not realise that your time, energy and thoughts are your greatest treasures. When you have learned to balance your times of activity and silence, when you take time to sit quietly, freeing yourself from all the outside influences, you will help yourself gain extra inner strength. Inner strength gives you a great power as you will have learned never to rush into unknown situations, helping you maintain your self-respect at all times. Self-respect and love for yourself is very important. You have to have these two qualities before you are really able to help others.

Always look for the love and good within others, and you will be saved from disappointments. All the people you meet in your lives are there for a reason, to teach you and to help you. Give them something to make them strong. We do not mean to give material gifts, but give of yourself to share your courage and peace, self-respect and enthusiasm for life. When you give all you meet these gifts, you will feel your heart overflow with love. This way you will always be special to all you meet and will be able to help everyone you meet on your life's path. Respecting and loving self, not in the sense of ego, but by focusing on your Creator God, life becomes lighter and richer spiritually.

Remember, be flexible and try to uplift all the people you meet. Being like this in all the situations you meet in life will be significant. You will be able to forget your past and enjoy the future. Remember friends, live every day to the full, remain content and kind. Then you will create opportunities for all those you meet. Because your nature is generous-hearted you will master a great lesson in life and always lighten the atmosphere wherever you go.

Please remember friends, each and every one of you is truly special to God. Never let mundane concerns make you false or superficial. Remember to hold to Truth and Love and you will learn from everything and everyone you meet. Enjoy the present! Be fearless, and you will be surprised how you will transform, realising that challenges come and go. When you become unhappy sit down in the quiet, remember God loves you. You are special, so do not let things get you down, think of what you have learned from the situation. If life is truly heavy, give all the worries to your Father/Mother God. Remember God will always help you. Remain free, remembering everything will work out for the best; just think about all the problems you have got through. We here in spirit always help with God's Will when your prayers of 'help' are sent to us. Remember always that you too are part of God. You are Spirit. Your own life is true proof of your own spirituality. Remember too that taking time to talk to God will keep you safe. No one can harm the true you.

God never ever forgets you, keep your faith. Be strong and fearless. See yourself as loved by God and you will develop strength to pass each of life's tests. But remember, stay humble, have love for all. See a good quality in everyone, and you will dance through life. People will find you wonderful to be with because you have the qualities needed to accept life amidst all its chaos. Truth and Love will help you move gracefully through all life's experiences, with inner strength. Remember God loves you.

In Spirit we watch you all remembering our earthly lives, understanding your problems. We hope you have gained insight from this message.

DEPRAVITY

Life is wonderful, such a glorious gift that your Mother/Father God gave you. Many of you take your gift for granted. You have lost your self-respect and purpose in life. You are wasting your life by being sucked into the lower debased ways of life.

Some of you have been easily led astray into the world of drink, drugs, violence and sleaze. Stop! Think what you are doing to yourselves, your loved ones, family and the people around you. They are so deeply hurt by your way of life and many are carrying your guilt for you.

Stop! Change now, seek help before you lose your soul completely. Regain your self-respect, you can do it, use the free will God gave you. There are many that will gladly give you their love and support to help you free yourselves from the ones who are leading you into the very pits of depravity.

Ask for help, pray to God, help will be given to you. You do not need to face this alone, your Father/Mother God never turns a child of theirs away. Just take that first tiny step and ask for help and it will be given.

FEEL THE BEAUTY WITHIN YOU

Everyone wishes to fit in with everyone around them, to be liked, respected and loved. But it is important in this lifetime that you do what you feel is right for you. Do not conform to others' wishes just to please them. God gave everyone of you free will, this is yours always. It is essential that you always honour yourself or you will be unable to respect or love self.

If you do not love yourself, and all your mistakes as opportunities to learn from, how will you be able to love anyone else? Give yourself unconditional love and be totally free to express yourself as you want. Always listen to your inner self, your conscious and do what you know is living your life as you are meant to. This is honouring self, loving and knowing your strengths and weaknesses and learning from them.

It is very important that in honouring yourself you respond to your inner feelings in each situation you meet. This is the way to move forward. It will not always make you popular, but if it feels right and follows God's laws, then it is correct for you. When you wish for approval from all, then you are prevented from being fully alive, loving, and honouring yourself. You will always be searching for the response you wish to see, feel, or hear from others. You will regret not having done things as your heart told you.

Look at the freedom of the wild animals, insects, birds and sea life. They use their inner instinct to live, and give life their best shot. Look at all the beauty around you. Feel the beauty inside you. This is God's Creation, life as you were meant to live. Feel the beauty of the life you were given, the free will to make the choice to follow your heart and your truth as you honour yourself and all of God's Creation. Do not waste such a precious gift. It is your life.

POWER

A great power is being brought to the earth plane to help all those who seek the Divine Truth. Those of you who understand the meaning of your earthly lives, and the purpose here on Earth need to help those who search for the Truth. Help them by answering their questions but do not preach to them for this will drive them away. Be kind, loving and compassionate towards everybody. Let them see your light glow and share in the love that you feel for yourself and all of Creation.

People are afraid of what they do not know or understand. Let them see by your way of life, that there is nothing to be afraid of and that your whole life and way of being is enriched by your beliefs. They will then open their hearts and minds to the Holy Spirit when they finally grasp the meaning of their lives.

Until you all understand the whole meaning of life there will be no peace within you or the world. You might say it is peace-time in some places, but not for all. There are always many wars of different sorts raging around the world. Some are to do with the materialistic ways of man and the many physical battles that go on all the time around the world, or the wars many have against diseases. These are all caused by the troubled minds of mankind for all the thoughts and ideas of negativity anywhere around the world at any moment, all of these affect the earthly body- the whole body of mankind, of which each of you are a part.

Once the majority of people have opened their eyes to the Holy Spirit's power, they too will believe in God and eternal life, as their vision will be cleared. Help all you meet in life. Enlist their hearts, minds and souls by setting an example of love, compassion, and true understanding. Remind them that material things are for sharing on the earth, that they cannot be taken with them when they pass over to Spirit. Remind them also that all the spiritual strengths gained whilst on earth as they learn their lessons and develop spiritual understanding, will be theirs eternally.

Step forward friends. Let your light shine out, so others gather round you to learn from your good thoughts and deeds, and to feel the warmth of the love you share so freely from your heart with all.

MATERIAL AND SPIRITUAL GIFTS FROM GOD

Often many ask questions such as, 'Why has he/she got so much more materially or spiritually than I have?' 'What have I done to deserve this life I have?'

Dear children, this is what you all are, Children of God. I want you to realise that God loves you all equally, and is not kinder to one than to another. Each one of you has the same opportunities in life, and all the same privileges. Your Mother/Father God knows all your troubles and shares your worries and sadness you feel. He is eternally around you giving you his love and support. You have chosen to come to Earth to learn and through life's challenges and opportunities.

Most of you here tonight have been honoured that the Master Christ has called you to serve others. You are blessed that you have that power to be able to respond to the calling. You must always aim to do good in order to exercise the power which God has given into you, so you that may help to awaken others when they too are ready. Many of you know that you have had countless lives in other worlds before you came here to the earth, to the body of flesh you now wear. You have had many earthly lives, and are now ready to be the truth-givers and peace-makers. You are all able to send out your powerful thoughts to the universe. Such thoughts of peace and harmony, enable those who are at war or in conflict with others, to feel a sense of love falling on and into them, perhaps making them feel a little calmer and less angry with others.

There are many situations in the world today that make your heart ache, but do not lose your faith. Be undaunted and help to quell the fears of others. Be the pioneers of peace, and one day it will be so.

You, children of God, the brothers and sisters of the Christ Jesus carry the light within you. Recognise the plight of your fellow beings, animals and plants. Send out the healing thoughts which they so badly need, keep hold of the Torch of Love and Truth, and stretch out your hands to all who need help.

Your Mother/Father God wishes that each one of you be as a miniature 'Christ' but, alas, the time goes on and only those who have learned to think, speak and act like Christ did when He walked the earth can do as 'Christ'. Do not be jealous of others. All of you are rich in an abundance of gifts from God. Use these gifts as you alone can, where and when they are needed. Always embrace all with an open, loving heart.

YOUR FUTURE

Many of you on the earth seek the help of people who read the Tarot, the stars, or numerology, in the hope you will find out your future fortune. All these methods are catering to your ego's illusion of life and will do nothing for the spiritual side of your unfolding and growth. Brothers, sisters, while you are on the earth, you continually have fear in your hearts concerning your future. It is your earthly mind, the ego's fear within you, fear of the unknown yet to come. Ego wants to keep a tight control on your life, it wants to be able to predict what is to come and be able to control the situation in your life. Your ego likes to weave a plot so that it can gain power over you and your personality. It wants to feel safe. Don't blame yourselves for this, for it is part of your lesson in life, learning not to let ego rule you. You really can't help yourself wanting to know what will come your way tomorrow, next week, next month etc., so instead of pushing ego away in judgement, put your trust and your ego anxieties in your Father/Mother God's hands.

Have you not realised yet friends, that if you knew what was to come, you would worry yourselves sick, until you met with the experience you had been dreading. Have you not learned by past experiences that you only come across problems with which you as a person can cope. These lessons are to strengthen your soul. This is why you are here. It is far better to live your life day by day, enjoying it. When a problem arises, deal with it then, and let it go once dealt with, to continue with your life- learning as you go forward without worrying continually about what may be around the next corner.

When you look back on the past, you always look back remembering what you call 'The good old days'. Yet you never seem to remember the challenges and the triumphs through which you have successfully learnt your lessons in the past. These challenges are very important in your life. They are your opportunities to learn.

Everyone has problems, worries, and what they think are great difficulties to overcome on their earthly journey. No one person is free of some worry or fear. All of you meet similar circumstances, but each of you reacts differently. This reaction will give a different outcome for each person. So you might think others couldn't possibly have the same problem or hardships. We assure you they do. Each of you has to live through Karmic or Universal Divine Law for the soul to progress. Each of you does this with your different personality qualities, strengths and weaknesses. Throughout your lives you face the same fears and experiences. A person who has gained spiritual insight has learned increasingly to let experiences come and go, knowing they are in the earthly school of learning, and that each problem solved is a step forward.

Remember friends, each of you chose your earthly life and the lessons it brings to you. We here know this is true, although you are not conscious of having done so.

Your ego is usually the cause of disharmony between the body and soul. This generates many stresses on the body through worrying. Responding to the earthly mind is not always a good thing, learn to recognise and feel your fear, then let it go-knowing it is not really real, that it has been manifested by the ego in an effort to control your life.

Whatever happens in your life, be grateful for all the experiences. Step into the moment, into the now, for this is the only important time in your life. Now is the moment to live. The past has gone and is no longer real or of importance to the real you, the spirit. The future has not come yet, there is always another tomorrow for you are eternal. You are creating your future now. Be fully present in each moment of your life. Feel yourself simply be in this moment, now. Learn by what you are doing, feeling, saying, hearing and seeing at this very time. Whatever you feel, be it hurt, happiness, anger, sadness, joy, be present and willing to learn from this experience, that is what you are here for. All moments pass you on to other experiences and you now know this. Move on friends. Remember that this life is not true reality, it is an illusion, a dream. Reality is the World of Spirit, where you all will return one day. Then you will see how well you learned your lessons. We here in the Spirit know it is not always easy to be kind to yourself, to look at your mistakes, acknowledge them and move on, but it is important to learn to do so.

It is impossible for you to know the future. It has not happened yet, so you only become aware of possibilities. So let your life unfold as it should, without any preconceived ideas of how you feel it will be. God knows your future. Leave all guidance to God. Listen to your true self within your heart. You can really do no more than listen to the Truth and react from your heart in ways that you feel to be right at that moment.

Your friends and loved ones in the World of Spirit will always help you as much as they are able, as will your guides. But you do need to ask for their help. At times of great stress and worry, remember the power of prayer to God. God will always answer you. Be patient, and know that it may not be as you expect, but He will answer with your best interests at heart. He will never let you down. So remember- live, love and be content and happy, friends. Do not continually try to peer round the next corner. It is not for since all truth will be revealed to you when your time is right.

LISTENING TO EACH OTHER

Friends, we wish to ask you all to pay more attention to other people's feelings and, importantly, to what they are talking about. Learn to listen to each other, do not comment or interrupt, do not agree or disagree, just be quiet and listen. The person is talking to you, expressing their thoughts, their feelings. It is so very important for them to be able to do this without interruption. When, and if, you are asked for an opinion, then yes, give one, but be very careful. If this is about their problem, a challenge for them to solve, then do not try to tell them what to do or say. Just underline the points they bring up, and you will find they have an idea of what they wish to do. Do not try to fix other people's problems. They have a different life to yours and your answer would lead to an inappropriate solution for them. Never try to fix people's lives, just be there for them. Be gentle, caring and loving to them, show them you care deeply and are willing to give them the time they so need.

Most of you would rather talk than listen. Your egos love to listen to self, to put self into the limelight. This you know is wrong, ego is unimportant and must be left aside to let the spirit self come forward and lead your way. If you let your spirit side come forward, you will see straight away what the person who has come to you really wants and needs. Do not judge another. No one can judge another person as they do not know or understand another person's life, and what lessons they have had to learn along the way.

Just keep an open mind, with your heart open also. Listen to them. You will hear the truth of that person speaking to you. This is a way of showing love to each other, and of honouring each other. It is a gift of love and complete acceptance to be able to listen to another, unselfishly. Learn this gift. It is a true treasure of the spirit. Offer each other this gift whenever you feel, hear, or see another needs you. Remember friends, it is what they have to say that is so very important, not your translation of what is being said. Put your thoughts completely out of the way, let your spirit help their spirit, this is a way of truth and love.

PERFECTION

You all crave perfection friends. On earth there is no such thing as the perfect life. Perfection is yours when you realise it lies deep within each of you, the perfect Spirit, God. The perfect part of you, the Divine spark is just waiting to burst into flame when you awaken to your true self- the spirit within the human overcoat.

All on earth is as it should be. There will never be the truly perfect life on earth. It is a learning plane of existence for all. Your life, as we have told you many times before, has been chosen by you. The lessons you wish to learn are now being learned. All, as we say, is as it should be. Nothing is perfect and nothing is permanent while you dwell on earth.

God in His kindness and love for you lets you make and choose your own lessons in your life. When you have passed through the wrong door along your pathway of learning a few times, you will have learned by the outcome that that direction is wrong for you. So next time you come up against this choice, you will have learned not to enter that door again and will pass the door to walk on to a different experience, which may be the choice you want this time around.

Many of you crave the beauty of the hair, face and body, and do everything you can to satisfy that craving through the power of using money to buy perfection as you see it. But if the soul within is mean, jealous, egotistic and cruel, then this will shine through. People will eventually see through this outward appearance of beauty and see the true ugliness of that person.

The beauty lies within you all. Let it out friends. Let it shine through you. People will see the love, compassion, care and generosity of your soul. As we have told you before, beauty is but skin deep. The beauty of spirit and soul is as Divine within you. This is the true beauty your hearts really crave for. Recognise this. The physical body will only be beautiful for a while. All things on earth grow old, deteriorate and pass on. When the time of the earthly person has passed on, it is your soul/spirit body that holds the beauty. Let this permanent beautiful, eternal and wise part of you, come through. Isn't this what you really desire, but haven't realised?

Open your hearts friends, to reality. Let God give you the gifts he wishes you all to have. Your Father/Mother God is unable to give you these gifts unless your heart and mind are open to his Love and Truth. Many of you crave the gifts of the Holy Spirit, which God gives by divine law. Some receive them a little earlier than others, because through the ages, they have gained from their earthly experiences, opening their hearts and minds to allow the Holy Spirit in. To receive them you must accept the responsibility of Love, Truth, Compassion and God's Will- the true purpose of your earthly life. Be courageous. Take the strength Spirit offers you. Bind yourselves together in love friends. Do not abuse the gifts and strength God gives you. Use them in selfless service to other. That is what their true purpose is. To help awaken all to bond together in True Unconditional Love- this is Perfection.

Remember God never says 'No' to you. All the problems of the world are made through the hands and minds of mankind. The mess is all yours. Remould the future, friends. Change it. Make it a better future for all living on earth- animal, vegetable, plant, fish, bird and man. The time to take responsibility for your lives is now. Remember God lets you do as you wish. You have total free will. Even if this takes you further away from your Mother/Father God for a time. Until Divine Law, Karma, eventually brings you full circle, back home into God's arms of Unconditional Love. Talk to God. He always listens. He always answers so listen when God speaks. Hear God, your inner higher self, your conscience as God speaking to you. Do what is right. You know what is said to you is true. You feel it in your heart and soul when it is right.

Try friends, to be perfect not just as you wish, but also as God wishes you to be. Remember God is Love.

BELIEFS AND SPIRITUALITY

Can one be spiritual and not go to Church, regular church goers often ask? Of course, a church or temple is a place where like-minded people meet to worship in faith. They believe and support each other in comradeship. To be spiritual is an inner experience which is lived every minute, every hour of every day, it is not an easy task, but going to a temple, church or meeting place, where one's religion is shared intimately is not necessary. Spirituality is the seed within a person, which grows at its own pace. Spirituality is seeing beauty everywhere. Perhaps while walking out in the fields, woods, or by the sea. Perhaps while sending out thankfulness to God for your life. Spirituality is living as good and tolerant a life as you are able.

Your church, or temple, is your earthly body. Mixing with others to commune with God is not necessary. You can do your own thing. Prayer need not take place in a building that is used for worship. In fact you should talk and pray to God as often as you can, and you can do this anywhere and at any time of the day or night. You just need a loving, accepting heart. A heart that accepts the religion of others, as well as being able to accept others as spirit, just like you, appreciating people as they are, respecting and loving them as fellow beings.

Spiritual people know that Love is the essence of life, and not religion. Love is the answer to all of life's problems, in fact, to the world's problems. Spiritual people do not blame others for their personal problems, or the problems of the world. They realise problems arise when people disconnect from God and from the seed of goodness within them.

Spiritual people are at peace with themselves. They are helpful and kind to all life on earth. You need to be disciplined to be peaceful, kind and tolerant to others. You need to be disciplined to pray and give grateful thanks to God often, wherever that may be, in a church, temple, field or car. The truth is that religion is often dogmas that disguise truth with narrow minded followers. It is time they opened their minds to the reality of life, and dropped their fear of other people's beliefs and way of life.

Religion is still causing problems on the earth, people are still being victimised or killed because their religion is different from another's. It is as though 'righteousness' has gone wrong- each believing that they are right, their religion is right and everyone else is wrong. Religion is unimportant. It is Faith that is important. Break the traditions of religious rigidity that destroys people. Regain pure faith in God, your God. Everyone has their own idea of what God is, this is their freewill. Yet there is but One God and all paths lead to Him, as we often tell you.

So, 'Can one be spiritual and not go to church?' Yes of course. You do not have to belong to a church to be spiritual. Open your heart to Love. Stay open-minded about others. It is really none of your business what others do or believe. Do not judge others. You do not know what their lives have held. Just take responsibility for your own life and spirituality. Stay connected to God in your own way. Remember your purpose in life. Interact lovingly with all life as Jesus showed you. Be guided by your inner God, not by human figures of authority. Be authentic. You are unique. What is right for others may not be right for you. We hope to have given you food for thought about your own life and views.

A SPIRITUAL PERSON

Many people think they are truly spiritual, but in reality it is a very rare quality to be truly spiritual. They deceive themselves into thinking that they are spiritual. These people often put themselves above other life on the earth plane. They think they are better people for attending a church, whatever denomination this may be.

A truly spiritual person never puts self first or above any other life. They know that all life is simply the energy of wholeness. All are universal beings. All are equally important to God and to mother Earth, and should be equal within your minds also. When complete understanding and total acceptance of every possible type of organism has been reached, then, yes, a spiritual consciousness is there.

We here in Spirit realise it is human nature to lie to others and to yourselves. But one of your first responsibilities is to be truthful to others and self, then you can live the Truth as God intended. True spirituality has to be worked at continually whilst you are on the earth plane. Remember to be true to your starting point. Walk forward with that Truth in your heart.

FEELING UNWORTHY

No-one is less important than another. God loves all His children equally. When you feel unloved or feel unworthy, remind yourself that you have all the love you will ever need inside you. Where? You ask. God's given you bounteous love inside your heart seed. It is the fear you have of life and what it holds for you that makes you feel unloved.

You are a good, worthy person in God's eyes, whatever you may have said or done. Things get out of hand when you feel fear, you have trouble staying connected to God, and then you believe that there is something wrong with you and you feel rejected by others. This is really just the fear within you invoking more fear. As this is a negative element it will simply bring more negativity towards you. This leads to you being afraid of being open and giving and receiving love, as you feel so bad about self.

Real love comes from deep within you, for you, from God's essence that is within you. Sit down and think of what we have told you, and break the negativity within you, go forward, knowing you are deeply loved, especially by God, and you will always be acceptable and lovable in His eyes.

When you find fault with yourself you will also find fault with others, and act on these feelings. Then you will be unable to look past appearances, and you won't recognise the person who wishes to give you love. Don't judge yourself so harshly and you won't judge others in the same harsh analytic way you have. You will then find that you will feel worthy again and feel more positive about life in general.

Go forward friends, you are all worthy, you are all perfectly lovable and truly, you are loved.

REWARDS

Many of you are committed to working actively in helping others to understand the full meaning of Life on earth. Do not be disappointed when people shy away from you. They are simply not ready to accept what you know, just yet. Things will change, but this will take time. There is much goodness in the world and the light of God will spread. Until this happens and people start to awaken, do not expect worldly approval, understanding and support.

The vibrations of the people on earth are very slowly being raised. People are full of goodwill, but are not ready just yet to accept the realisation of communication with the Spirit world. Remember each one of you subconsciously walks along a self-appointed path of life. Our blessings from the spirit world are shining down on all of you. We are trying to gently guide you along your righteous pathways.

People of the world, do not fret about the troubles that spring up around the world. Keep your faith and confidence in your God, He/She has a Divine plan at work. Remember all things that happen are the law of cause and effect. God is Love, remember this, it is difficult for many to realise this when they look to see what is going on around the world. All things are out-workings of love, even if it does not appear to be so.

Remember friends, communities in other countries are following the pathway they have made for themselves by the Law of Affinity. All people all over the globe are treading their pathways, although sometimes painful and sad to see. All people must learn to develop tolerance and a greater understanding of others in the world. The Christ Light is bringing light to areas where there is darkness. It may seem that that light is making the darkness more easily visible. Your prayers to send love, light and healing reach those areas of the world, and we in spirit wish to give you thanks for sending your prayers to these regions.

When you pass to the world of spirit you will have a greater understanding of the spheres of life and of how thought and unconditional love are the true creative powers. Life, we know gets very confusing for you at times because of your level of vibration at this time. Raise your level of consciousness and inner knowledge to help expand and raise the minds of your friends, family and acquaintances.

Those of you who understand the true teachings of Jesus Christ will often experience the disdain of others because at this time they only understand materialistic ways of the world. Be patient, hold them all in love. People will soften to your views as they see that the life you lead is one of love and acceptance of all others. Committed yourself to God, and you will receive spiritual rewards, and only spiritual rewards will pass with you into the realms of spirit. Do not resent material success. Show others how to be content with what you have, and show compassion to others in need.

God gives spiritual rewards of happiness, and opportunities to serve mankind with great inner peace. All of you have God's gifts and your reward is becoming aware of ways to use them for the good of the 'Whole'. Embrace His gifts with love and without expectations, working with Truth, Love and Compassion for all.

SERENITY

People look for serenity in many places. They seem to think they will find this gentle, mild, emotion somewhere around them. Perhaps even gain this placidity through someone else, somehow!

No! True serenity is earned through life's many lessons. It comes from deep within a person, from deep, deep down, from your soul, from your own spirit.

When you truly know your life's purpose you will have found that serene, even tempered spirit within yourselves. You will have a great love for your Creator and all life.

Serenity is a feeling of deep inner peace. A calm understanding of why and what you are on earth for. It comes from the Christ Spirit deep within you. Something you cannot buy or find in the material world.

Try to find that inner calmness. It comes when you feel peaceful contentment within your own life.

This collected composure and peace of mind is present once you have found your God within. True tranquillity and stillness, almost sedateness is felt deep within your heart. It is a sensation of inner peace. It is a stillness that is so elusive that it may take a lifetime to find. Unfortunately many never do seem to find this feeling of serenity.

Take time out to be alone with your God. Talk to Him. Learn to be Godlike in speech and action. The world will soon look a better place and your purpose will surely be found. Have faith, friends.

WINTER MONTHS

So many people get very low in the darker months of the year.

Remember nature needs this darker time to recuperate and to germinate seeds of new life and growth.

All things created need rest, just as the Lord rested on the seventh day of creation.

This is essential. Then life is refreshed with new zest and colour.

When you are feeling low, look around you. Realise it's just a resting time for all life, including human life.

People often do not realise just how much in tune all life is, animal, plant and human.

Everything around them has a low energy in these resting months. This is the way of nature and life.

Lift your thoughts up to the higher realms, to your Father/Mother, to the glorious life- giving power of light and love.

This will fill you with strength anew and you will feel the refreshment you need to carry on stepping forward.

God Bless each one of you.

HEAVEN HELPS THOSE WHO HELP THEMSELVES

These, my friends, are true words, one has to have the will to get oneself up and going, whatever situation is around you.

Always stay positive. This will help you get through the difficulties you come across in your lives. Difficult situations will always arise. You are on the earth plane to learn. All these difficulties are your lessons. No one has an easy time on the earth plane. All have their own trials, troubles, worries, and conflicts. Each person deals with their life as their circumstances will let them, as they feel is right at that precise time. No one should try to tell another how to live, think or act. You are all individuals, with free will, people living life and learning from their lives, so that their soul can grow.

Your earthly lives are for living, learning and giving. By giving we mean giving of your self, of your time, love and compassion, and being tolerant of all.

Start each day with a heart full of love to share with all you meet. Give something of yourselves to everyone you meet. Perhaps you can give a helping hand, a smile, a little understanding or a listening ear. Just do your best each day, your heart will fill to overflowing and fulfilment in life will be yours.

You all owe it to yourselves to do the best for all life and for your planet. It is to your advantage.

When your time comes to return home to the World of Spirit, you will pass over knowing you have given your best to all. On reflection upon your individual lives you will see just how much you have accomplished. Not materially perhaps, but through humanitarian love for your fellow life forces on the planet.

Friends, we continually tell you love is the way forward to all aspects of your lives. Many of you still find this hard to comprehend Love is the Power Source of all Life. Listen all of you, it is deep in yourselves. It is the essence of your very being. Let it flow and engulf you and all you do, say and think.

No one said Life was going to be easy. How could you learn if it was? Embrace your life. Do your best, and as long as you do, you will be helping all life, including yourself.

GOD LOVES YOU ALL EQUALLY

Friends, people on the earth plane build a wall between themselves and God. How do they do this? Sometimes through feeling unlovable and separated from love. Sometimes through wrong actions and thoughts like greed, deceit, envy, pride, jealousy and lust. Stop, look and listen to yourselves.

Your Mother/Father God loves you all dearly, but by cutting yourselves off from God with these thoughts and actions, you cannot feel the unconditional love with these thoughts and actions, you cannot feel the unconditional love sent to you every second of the day and night. God loves you, it doesn't matter who you are, or what you are, God loves all His children equally. Your Father/Mother God would never desert you. No one is too bad or too good. Everyone is loved completely. All of you are important to God. Each and every one of you are known and loved. Whatever your strengths and weaknesses everyone is important. Good or bad, you have important life experiences to share with each other. Just start each day afresh and face God. He will always welcome you with open arms and assist you to learn from your weaknesses and mistakes. Every one of you needs God. Your lives will be much better when you open your heart to God and let your love flow to Him, to yourself and to all life. Allow yourself to receive His love and your love for yourself and the Divine in you.

Remember God never judges you. He is Love, always there for you. Make your life worthwhile. Do not waste it. It is a short time that you are on the earth. Make the most of this time, so that when you return home again to spirit, you have many life experiences you can share with all there.

Remember you are all part of the 'Whole', and your experiences on the earth benefit every spirit and soul. You all learn so much from each other, learn to love all life, you cannot be parted from any of God's creations, all life is One.

If you hurt another in any way this will eventually return to you. Remember too, that if you are kind and good to others in life, this also will be returned to you.

Friends, take heed of these words, and go forth each day with your best foot forward, ready to love and serve one another.

Discover the real Truth of your lives. The reality of knowing God, and trying to live life as his one son Jesus did, remember he who believes in Him shall not die but shall have life eternal.

AGE OF AQUARIUS

Brothers and sisters, the New Age of Aquarius is upon you. Keep Christ in all your hearts, as the future depends on all of you. The existence of your planet depends on your thoughts and actions, which are your responsibility. The new age is here. My friends, lead a physical life where you are like an instrument, inspiring harmony in your daily lives. Bring the Love of Christ from deep within you into all you do and say. Help all you meet with a deep felt compassion, so that others see your inner peace and spirituality towards them. Let your Christ Light catch and alight the spirits of others, this way you will see the darkness on the earth disperse, so that your world shows that the Christ Power is with you all, shining from the tiny planet earth out into the universe for all to see.

Focus always on the Love, the unconditional love that God sends you. This will keep you strong and help you lift your thoughts, preventing you feeling low. Have confidence in yourselves and in the events of your life. Remember they all have a greater purpose than you can understand. All that happens is part of God's Divine Plan. All that occurs in life is the result of cause and effect, and this is the result of the law of God's love. Keep your confidence in the Lord your God, and know that God who is Love, has a greater love, greater tolerance, and a greater understanding of how to bring the light through the material world's darkness.

Guard your thoughts people of the earth. Remember, thoughts become reality. Thoughts control matter, Project your spiritual thoughts of healing, love and light out through the spheres of all Creation. This way, the simple powerful essence of life, divine love, will radiate out to all, uplifting the whole world, uplifting all into the wondrous light of the Lord God, pulling up also the lower planes of life and shedding light and love into darkness. This will help every soul to rise above their own limitations and confusion, letting them see what the darkness really is, helping them to choose the light, the way of Love. All worlds are evolving now in this new Age. They are responding to God, to the light of the Christ Spirit. Look forward through this new Millenium.

ARMAGEDDON

Friends, this is a very important message that we would like you to listen to.

Stay positive about your future, about the world's future. There is no doom and gloom ahead for mankind.

Do not listen to the prophets of doom, they have always been around. Overcome your fear and ignorance about the millennium you are entering. This is a time of awakening for mankind. People of the world are now more compassionate towards others than ever before. They feel love and compassion for others in countries where there is war and conflict. People are aware of the problems all life has on mother Earth, and of the damage mankind is inflicting on her.

The light of Christ is deep within all of you. It is becoming more potent and shedding healing encouragement. Positive changes are starting to happen all around the world.

People have a great desire for peace. They wish to avoid confrontations with other countries, now more than ever before. People know now that confrontations are the wrong way to resolve world differences. People want more diplomacy among countries. Look at all the people who are now aware of the plight of animals and of plant life on the earth. People are fighting to make others aware of the need to take better care of mother Earth and all her inhabitants.

There are people who spring up out of nowhere, spreading negativity, fear and doubt among you. It is your choice if you wish to listen to them and build your future with these fears in your hearts and mind.

Free will is always yours, friends, but here in the world of spirit we ask you to have tolerance, confidence, and only good, kind thoughts every day. This is important. Be optimistic, positive and feel joyous about the future. This will create a future which will heal the conditions around the world and lift the global consciousness of mankind.

Love, as we always tell you, is the Greatest Power mankind will ever know. Let it emanate in your hearts, helping humanity join together as one, raising the vibration of human consciousness.

The future of the earth is good, far more people than ever before are now aware that thoughts are powerful things. So many people understand that by controlling your thoughts you can control the world you personally live in.

Prophecies always come at significant dates. The media, television, the press, etc. love stories of doom and gloom. Good news rarely makes your headlines. Look at the predictions, the thousands of predictions in the past, which never came to anything.

'Armageddon' is about to happen, but not on the material level. Spiritually things will continue to evolve in man. This is a time of conflict, war, between the lower self of mankind and the higher heart and mind of mankind. It is a time of progress for mankind, to be more aware, more open minded. This is a time when mankind will be more compassionate and each will open up their heart to others.

You have all always had free will, so now it is up to you. What thoughts do you wish to pour out each day? Positive thoughts can enlighten the world and push love and wisdom forward in humanity?

When you do succumb to feelings of fear and depression, realise you are not doing yourselves or the world any good. Create some good, positive thoughts. Realise these are constructive thoughts of light, love and harmony.

We here see one vast brotherhood in the future. It is a brotherhood that loves all God's creatures and cares for the Earth. We see a world of peace, beauty and harmony.

Hold on to these thoughts friends, and look forward to the future and all it brings, knowing God's ultimate Divine plan is well underway. Man is learning his lessons well and progress is good.

SELFISHNESS AND SACRIFICE

Friends, when the spirit is in the earthly body, it has a compulsion to protect and nurture self first. It is a survival instinct. Unfortunately it can become a fault. What was meant to help a person survive is often turned by the individual into selfishness and greed, a wanting of everything one sees or hears about. It turns into greed so often and so easily. Selfishness is best avoided as soon as you realise this is what you are guilty of.

Many others sacrifice everything they have, including their own safety for others around them. Materials things are not important for this type of soul. Then you have many people who, as a matter of course, try to save, scrimp, and even hoard, for their offspring, so they have life easier than they did.

All these attributes are natural to human nature, it is all these together, a little of each, in fact all things taking, giving, saving, in moderation. Balance is what is called for, if the scale tips too much one way then strive to adjust the balance within yourself and the way you live your life.

Service is an aspect of sacrifice also, but to God and fellow man, animal and plant life. Remember that the true meaning of sacrifice it to make sacred. Here is really the only place where there is certainty of gaining that inner peace of mind. Remember material possessions only have their uses on the earth plane. It is the many treasures of the spirit that is of value for man and all life forces. We understand it is hard to get the balance right. We here in spirit, have also had to learn this way of the earthly form.

Remember friends, all young need clear boundaries, so they can eventually learn self-control of mind and body and do not go overboard in one direction or another.

Yes, sacrifice associated with service to others and to God gains spiritual rewards, but you are of the earth. You are here also to enjoy your life and to learn in your daily life. Then, when you pass to the other side of life, you will have learnt balance in all things, and learnt the balance of the many emotions you came to experience and learn.

INSPIRATIONAL THOUGHTS

Inspirational thoughts come and go, so fleetingly, softly do they flow gently through our hearts and minds, from loving Spirit Guides by our side.

They try so hard to teach the way for us to live here on this earth, easiest ways for us to learn, to step upward to meet our heavenly Parent.

To rejoin our whole family of Life in love, harmony, and eventually to become the whole rejoined with our Creator as intended.

Such little is asked of us, for all we have been given on this beautiful world. Love, harmony, peace, trust, truth, compassion, for all of life and loyalty to our God, whoever we may think she/he is. For all good ways are Godly and lead to the same God.

This my friends, is all that is asked of us, let us try a little harder each day to accept each other as we are, so once more we can become 'One'.

PERSONAL BELIEF

Religion is the belief system of a group of people who share the same beliefs and values. It is the belief of the individual being which is crucial to your evolution. The word religion can mean what sect, organisation or denomination you belong to and can indicate what you believe in. Everyone is entitled to their own personal belief whatever it may be. It is the spiritual being within the body that impresses that person to follow their own religion, to choose their own understanding of God.

When you pray, you talk to the energetic being, the Spirit being that is infinitely wise and loving, that one being in whom you believe. It is the anchor of human life to believe in something. Most people are aware of the omnipresence of God. They have a knowing that God, the Great Creator of all life is everywhere and present at and in everything at the same time. Most people accept this great intelligent power that has created all life and the Universes. It may be all too much at times to understand what type of power this may be that knows all, sees all, and feels all. It is baffling for human minds to realise that type of presence that is around and within you all the time.

When you go home to the world of energy and spirit, your mind will awake and you will regain the understanding of God, that you have always really had deep within you. You will know it was of no importance what name you gave God, or which God you prayed to or worshipped, as all roads lead eventually to the One Great Almighty Divine Creator, as we have told you many times before.

Remember just to allow others have to have the belief that is right for them in this lifetime, just as you have yours. Tolerance of others and their beliefs is very important.

Keep to the laws of life, creation and spirit in this universe. The laws of the land are important, for without law and order life on earth, or any other place in the vast universe of life, would not be possible.

Accept that which you find acceptable in your heart, and know this is right for you, no one else, just you. Never force any of your beliefs on another. Each one of you has God within you which we call the Christ Light. You have been told this by many spiritual teachers. This divine essence is in all life. All of you have this God goodness inside you. Perhaps in some of you, that goodness has not yet surfaced, but it will when the Soul/Spirit has reached that stage of evolution. Each one of you evolves at a different speed and along different paths.

Free will has been, and always will be, yours for you to choose how you live and think in your life. Lives (of which you all have had a great many, although you may not be aware of this, or even believe this), make for the growth and progression of the Soul through a sequence of lives.

People, friends of the earth, the message we wish to give you is to be compassionate, and tolerate each other, also each other's beliefs. You can learn a lot from each other's beliefs. Do not close your minds, there is truth hidden in all things. Really it is none of your business what belief another person has, you have a life of your own, and a lot of development of soul to bring about in self, so what others think should not be your concern. Leave other's lives to them. If another asks your views on life then, yes, give your belief, but do not belittle another's beliefs. Tell them how your way of life and your God helps you, but that is all. Never, we repeat, never, try to force your views or beliefs on anyone else. Beliefs and opinions are not really important. Actions hold the key, so do your best for all forms of life throughout your life. If you insist that your views and beliefs are the only right ones and that any other belief is wrong, then 'righteousness' has gone wrong and conflict is created.

When a person says, "When you die you are dead, and this is the end", after his transition, when his loved ones taken him home to the World of Spirit, their mind will awaken to the infinite love of God, and to what the purpose of life was and is all about. What is important, as we have said, is the way you live your lives. Treat life, all life, with the respect and love you would like to be given to you. Be open to receive such love from yourself and others as you live your life using the life force within you for the highest good of all.

People who try to turn others against their beliefs, do the most damage. They destroy the faith of others and prevent their personal soul growth.

There is One 'God'. It really does not matter to whom you pray. Talk to whoever you feel is in your heart, whoever you can accept and respect as infinite love and wisdom. It is faith that makes your life truly feel worthwhile and have a purpose. All pathways lead home to the One Almighty Creator, the One whose essence you all have and which is part of everyone and everything. Enjoy your life, be considerate. Treat all life with unconditional love, as your God loves you. Respect life, then you will be respecting God. Love one another, then you will be loving God also.

We leave you to reflect on our words to you, and remember God is the Infinite Love, whoever you think He is.

A PRAYER FOR ALL

Dear Lord

We here humbly ask for help for all the people in troubled areas of the world.

Please help the leaders of these countries to see sense and bring peace to all under their rule.

Help all those people and animals who are suffering in the world where natural disasters are causing pain and havoc.

Please help us all to understand the way Spirit works here on earth, for there are times when things appear to be harsh on the innocent.

We are grateful for the divine, unconditional Love and care, given freely to all on earth.

The healing to all who are sick in hospital beds, institutions and homes is very gratefully received.

Help each one of us to think more like you, to talk as you would, and to act in our daily lives just as you would Lord.

Amen

PRAISE THE LORD

Praise the Lord
Creator of All
Large and small
From the Cosmos to the tiniest microbe

Created from Love was all
God is this Love

God is in all
Love is in everything
As God is part of his creations

Love is all around
Love is Power
Use this Power for the world's advancement of all the spirit creations
Praise our Lord of Love

CHRISTMAS TIME

Angels call
Angels shout
What's it all about?

Give food
Give shelter
Give help
Give love
What? You are not able?

'The cost, the cost!'
We hear you shout
Money, money, is all that counts
Life is ten a penny.

Help others!
'No, not us,
For we are not able.
Our money is needed for us
To set our table.'

See others shudder,
Hear them shout.
Is that all life is about!

CHRISTMAS

Christmas time is here once more
How many remember the tiny baby born so long ago.

Jesus came to show us all how
To live graciously and with kindliness.

All this is now forgotten by so many
In their rush for material comforts.

TRUST IN SPIRIT

Trust yourselves to divine spirit more.
Let go of self. Relax, be still.
The essence of life is Spirit
God is Spirit.

Spirit is always with you,
Around you and within you.
Stop a while, listen.
Silence is the essence of the Soul.

All of life is Spirit.
So solid all may seem,
But please remember
Life is but another dream.

Reality exists when earthly
Life is left behind.
Back home in the World of Spirit
You will be
Reflecting on the dream
You left behind.

LISTENING

Fast and furious words should flow,
Teaching you all you know.

Like minds seek out minds,
Minds like their own.

Speak to each other,
Telling all you know.

Listen to others talking,
Hear every word.

Most of you don't hear the message

Try again and see what a difference
It can make for you.

IN HIS HANDS

A tap on the shoulder, you might feel
An angel of the Lord is he.
Turn, and you will see
Gentle as a lamb is he.

He who leads you and me,
Guides us so tenderly
Gently by the hand.
Lord of all,
It is good to be
Held in your hands
So lovingly.

MIDDLE OF THE NIGHT

Middle of the night
No bird songs fill the air.
Only owls hoot and screech
Man and nature are fast asleep.

Day breaks
Man and nature awake.
No bird songs fill the air.
Machines drone, drone, drone,
Drowning out nature's sound.

LISTEN

Listen, all you leaders of the lands
Listen to the spirit calls,
Listen to all they say
Listen to the Lord they cry
Listen and let him come alive inside,
Feel his gladness for all the world.

SPIRIT IN US

Our Father, Mother God
Divine Spirit in each and every one of us
Help us all to act purely out of love towards one another.
Help us to keep our ego out of all we do.
Help us to do all things for God in Service to all around us.

Selfishness is one of our greatest downfalls
So many times we put Self first.
How can we learn to give unselfishly?
So much we receive when we give from the heart.

We ask for a Blessing
Our Father, Mother God,
A blessing for mankind,
And the animal kingdom, sea life and plant kingdoms.

Amen

ANOTHER DAY

You have all died many times
You have all have seen
Every type of sorrow, joy and happiness.

After every storm there is always calm.
Keep your head held high in hope
for another day.

Know that all bad things and difficulties
Will pass away,
For you to see the beauty of life once more.

Keep your faith strong at all times.
Do not be distracted by
Troubles of the world around you.

The wise person accepts all with love.
Have the determination to keep on,
Keeping on.

Be silent inside yourselves and out.
The ultimate medicine is silence
Healing and strengthening the soul.

Listen to God each day while in prayer
Practise what you preach to all.
Always be truthful in all you say and do.

LET OUT YOUR SORROW

Let out your sorrow.
Let out your pain.
Let all know of your loss.

Take time to grieve.
Take time to heal.
Receive the love brought to you.

Know your loved ones live on.
Know they are loved.
Know spirit cares for them all.

Live your lives.
Live life to the full.
Live knowing you will meet again.

All who love meet again.
All are drawn together in love.
All need courage in the early days of loss.

God gives all life.
God lets all live eternally.
God will keep all spirit safe and loved.

PRECIOUS

Precious is the life you have,
Chosen by you. You know
Free will is your right on earth.
You choose the body, the brain, the life you wish to lead.

Everyone is equal. All are loved, just the same.
No one judges what you do or what you say.
Mother, Father God treasure each child,
No matter what the life they have lead has brought to them.

A LIFE SO YOUNG

You are hurting deep inside
No one knows how much
Another day feels just too much to bear.

Speak to your loved ones
Let them help you with their love
Through the loss of your kin.

Deprived through their death
Of love you felt was yours
Feelings of destruction overwhelm you.

God, you feel has robbed you,
Has stripped away the life so young.
Losing them leaves you raw inside.

Hold your head high and know that
Whatever may happen, you will continue
To fly forward on your journey.

Just keep on through each moment, each day,
Though only darkness seems ahead
You too will heal, the pain will ease.

Stop demanding more of your self.
Simply be at peace, enabling you to
Carry on until you meet your loved one once more.

Be courageous and flexible.
You can do anything you want, for
God will always be at your side.

WISDOM

Rough seas!
Gale force winds!
Blizzards!
Great trees bow down,
Respecting the powerful love of the Great Spirit
Knowing he is showing his mighty strength
For reasons known to him alone.

REMEMBER

Remember now that each life you have lived
Is moulding your soul and your spirit.
Through Karmic laws, you are the product
Of all the past lives that you chose.
Your experience and responses in the life you now live,
Mould the spirit through which you return.
For each time you will choose
How you wish to progress in each of your lives.
After rest and reflection, you will choose your next schooling
In new physical form. Then you start life on earth once more.

DRY YOUR TEARS

Dry your tears
Do not weep for me
I am here by your side.

Each tear you shed
I cry too
Though you are unaware of me.

Feel the tender breeze
Flow through your hair
And Brush against your cheek.

It is I trying to comfort you for
Love never forgets or dies
It lives forever just like you and I.

REFLECTIONS

Reflections of the day and night are you.
Remember you are spirit and soul clothed
Though a heavy robe you wear.
Not for long are you here.
Time will come, time will pass.
Then you'll drop the prison garment,
Light like the breeze you'll be!
Use the time, though heavy on the earth.
Greater knowledge you'll never learn again.
All wisdom you have gleaned from here you will share
With all those you love back home.
Do your best to spread the word
To all you know, and to those you don't.

WHAT IS GOD?

What is God? You ask
Who is God? You ask again.
God is Light and Dark
God is Spirit.
God is Love and Truth.
God is Peace
God is good
God is in all life.
God is the breeze that brushes your face
God is the rain and the hailstone,
God is the wind and the gale.
God is the snow and the ice,
God is the cloud and the thunder.
God is the star and the universe,
God is the moon and the night,
God is the sun and the day.
God is the tree, the flower, the weed and corn in the field.
It is far easier to say what is Not God!
God is the air you breathe, the earth you walk on.
Remember to give thanks to GOD.

DARK AND BRIGHT

Dark blue skies above
Overhanging grey clouds,
Tiny wet drops upon our face
Reflecting sunlight, with bright
Rainbow colours arcing above.
These are promises of sunny days ahead.

Life can be dark and blue,
Emotions overcast and grey.
Glimpses of light and joy
Are in each new morning dew,
Gleaming with colours, bright and light,
Promising that happy days will come to you.

OPEN UP YOUR HEART TO LOVE

Open up your heart to Love!
What changes you'd all feel!
With turmoil and hate erased,
Anxiety and worries would melt away.

Love is the essence of you all!
Open up your heart to Love!
Let it embrace your being and soul
Open minds will come then too so
War and strife, will be no more.

Love is the essence of all Life!
Pink hues of Love would surround your world.
Golden light of your Spirit home
Would make the whole world glow.

NEW LIFE OF LIGHT

Step into your new life of light and love.
Know that in love-light you are fully protected from the realms of spirit and evil.
Ask for all the help you need and it will be given.
Be patient in life, for time is on your side and all will come to those who wait.
Keep your faith and love for God, and all will work out for the best in your life.
Live by God's laws of love. This is all that is asked of you, to give love and service to one another.
Stay humble and true to your purpose in life. Once you have found your pathway, do not falter from it.
Tread lightly onwards for God will always carry you in times of difficulties and need.
He will never turn His back on you.
Let God shine His love-light on you as you walk forward on the pathway home to Him.

INTERTWINE

Our Father/Mother God
Who is all around and within us,
Please help heal all who are sick,
And all who are lonely.
Give them all the strength they need
For their daily lives.
Help us Lord to understand and care for
Our animal companions,
Better than we have in the past.
Let us all remember that
All creations of life are
All ONE.
We are each intertwined with each other.
Teach us to be patient and love one another, Lord.

Amen

DEAR GOD

Birds, bees and butterflies fly so delicately by.
Help us to be kind and good each day
So Angelic wings may help us sleep.

Amen

WAKEFUL

Ever wakeful do we wait
For our Saviour to descend
Among us once again.
Teaching all as he taught once before
To love
To care
To help all whom we meet,
Every plant, every animal or human.
Will we listen?
We will!
But will we do as he bids us?
Let us hope we all have more sense than before!

GUIDE US PLEASE

Guide us please heavenly Father,
Help us your children on the earth.
There is so much unrest everywhere

Help us with your Loving Guidance to put all wrongs to right.
To heal the sick, feed and clothe the poor
To take better care of Mother Earth and all life forms she supports.

Help us to spread thy word of
Love far and wide in whole
Truth as you would have us do, Lord.

Amen

HEALING PRAYERS

We send out healing prayers Lord,
To all wherever they are
On the street, at home
Or in a hospital bed.
Please grant them sweet and peaceful sleep tonight.
Grant healing to those who feel unloved.
Let them feel your love enfold them.
Those who are lonely, perhaps depressed,
Give them the upliftment they so need.
We thank healing Angels for all they do for us.
Keep us safe Lord on each of our journeys home.

Amen

❧❦

DEAR CREATOR

Dear Creator,
Give us knowledge
Of birds and insects of the sky,
Of sea life in the oceans deep,
Of plant life, rich and green for our animals on earth to eat.
Give us knowledge
So all may thrive.
Help us to learn to keep air, land and sea,
Clean, clear and fresh for Mother Earth,
So all can sleep in peace.

Amen

❧❦

PRAYER FOR A CHILD

Lord please lead us tenderly, every second of the day
So we may work and play, in the most righteous way
Work and play, we know we must
But in thee Lord God we put our trust

Amen

HELP ME SLEEP

Dear Lord,
Help me sleep
Help me count those fluffy sheep
To dream sweet dreams
To wake afresh
Ready for another day

Amen

EACH AND EVERY DAY

God help us each and every day
To do the best we are able.
Giving kindness all around and
Work to set our table

Amen

LISTEN

Listen, all you leaders of the lands
Listen to the spirit calls,
Listen to all they say
Listen to the Lord they cry
Listen and let him come, alive inside,
Feel his gladness for all the world.

PRAYING THOUGHTS

Brothers and Sisters all prayers
Your Father/Mother knows,
And everything you feel deep within yourselves for all those around you.
Each time you think kind compassionate thoughts of others, God knows.

We here in Spirit hear all your true heartfelt wishes.
You often worry, unnecessarily, about what you may have missed,
Or whom you may have missed out of your prayer, yet
God knows all of these.

Just by being thankful for all you have, and for all your life lessons,
Just by having good thoughts and doing all you can for others,
Is really all your Divine Parent wishes-
Just like any parent is proud of their giving, sharing, loving child.

A short prayer is often all you need to send in thought
(as we have told you, God knows all),
Just thank God for life,
Just ask for help for the lonely, the sick and bereaved,
And for those in transition from one life to another.

Just ask for the whole of God's Creations
To be given the healing love they need,
Just ask for universal peace.
This is truly sufficient.

FLY UP INTO THE SKY

Be loving and giving of yourself.
Be true to yourself.
Fly high with your new found wings,
Up into the Celestial sky,
Soaring like an eagle flying by.

KARMA

Emotions of life, love, hate, sorrow and joy,
Tears, and laughter.
All each spirit must know.
Giving, taking, good and bad,
God-like wisdom all to be had.
Young babies, old women and men,
None can escape this Karma law.
Hunger, thirst, greed and remorse, selfishness and wisdom,
Each of these, whilst on earth we shall have.

MOTHER EARTH

Mother Earth
Birds light as a feather
Elephants heavy as rock.
Mother Earth
Delight in all life together.

SECRETS

Birds, bees, flowers, trees,
Grasslands, deserts, ice and seas;
Hills, mountains, woods and glades,
Oh what secrets they all hold!
Only the Lord thy God would know.

STARS

Stars shine so brightly in the midnight sky,
Like sparkling sapphires they shine.
Thank him!
Praise him!
Make him smile.
God made these for you and I.

A DAY

Morning wakes us
Daytime breaks
Work, play
Tired at the end of the day.
Night time falls
Sleepy heads lay
Loving us all ,
Every watchful is our Father now.

EGO

Ego has every man
Keep it small as you can

Earthly soul, ego seeks
Do not let your ego speak

Spirit of the heart come forth
Squash that ego now and for all.

HEAL THE SICK

Heal the sick
Heal the soul
Heal the person as a whole.

Look at them
Frail and meek
Following each other
Just like sheep.

Help them stop to
Look around to
Ask the Lord
To make them strong.

ANCIENT ONES

Civilisations come and go
The Ancients are back to lend us a hand.
Let them guide you and take you forth.
Let not sorrow steal your strength,
Fight for right,
For justice and kindliness from now on
For all creations of the Lord.

LIFE

Life's work is never done.
Life goes on and on.
Each cycle, newness
Springs before you,
Beauty for you all galore.
Make the most of all,
Be sure God wants joy for all.

COLOURS

Colours light, colours dark,
Every colour holds its magic power.
Each one calls the person in need of its
Particular healing power and strength.

Colours gleam, colours glisten,
Colours drab or dull as mud,
Each one is really beautiful in its own right.
Each one has its own God-given power,
Each one is for us to draw upon.

Wake up you people of the world!
Open your eyes and see the glorious beauty
All around you every second of the day.
Then you will see what we say is true.

GREAT SPIRIT

We ask for help for
All animals in testing centres
Around the world.

Let us stop this cruelty.
May we treat all, whether large or small
With the love and respect they so deserve.

Let us treat all your creations
With the love and respect
We would like for ourselves.

We thank you God for
All the love and compassion
You give each and every one of us.

Amen

CHILD'S PRAYER

Dear God
Keep me sweet and kind Lord
At work and play,
Kind to others every day.
Please protect me while I sleep.

Amen

GENTLE JESUS

Gentle Jesus who helped the Blind,
Made all well, so they could tell
Of the miracles that befell.

Master Jesus help us to speak
To tell others, all their
Faith to keep.

Amen

TO GROW NEARER TO YOU

Dear Mother/Father God
We do not always appreciate all the things you have given us.
Forgive us please, we are like ungrateful children,
Who have all we need, but still we ask for more.

Thank you for the air we breathe,
For the world, the universe and all within God,
For our lives, our families and all our friends,
For the animal kingdom, our animal companions,
For our food and beautiful plants, the flowers and trees.

We wish also to thank the spirit world,
The angelic realms and elementals for all they do for us.
We cannot possibly imagine
How much help and support they give us.

We wish to lower our heads in thanks,
To be able to expand our spirit while here on earth
So as to grow nearer to you, the Creator of all life.
We praise and love you God.

Amen

HELP ALL

Give us strength Lord to fight
All dark areas in the world.
Let us have extra strength to
Bring the light and love to all
We meet whoever they are.
Let us not judge another person,
But see the Christ Light
Deep within them all.
Help all to let their light shine out brightly.

Amen

WE ASK ONCE MORE

God, we ask once more
For leaders of the world to see sense,
To stop the fighting,
To realise love is the only way forward.
Please give them the insight to realise
That wars must go now,
Not in the distant future,
When more lives are lost.

All wish for peace,
Let us all pray to you daily for love and
peace so the world looks like a
pink world of love from afar.
We thank you Lord for all our gifts.
We ask for help for all the sick,
the bereaved. Those who are in
transitions between this world
and the next. For all those in
the trouble spots of the world,
help them, give them the courage
they need to keep going.
Bring them peace.

Amen

WE ARE LIGHT

We are light,
We are dark
We are as old as the Ark.
Never do we learn to think,
Before we engage to speak.

Help us Lord, to do no wrong,
to think like you
to speak like you,
to act out our lives,
as you would have us do.

Amen

HELP THE LEADERS

God please help us to help those in need.

Help the leaders in the wealthy countries,
To realise that their duty and privilege is
To help all those in poorer countries.

Help the leaders to learn to tolerate
Other countries' traditions and also their religions.
Let them learn to love all the peoples of the world equally.

Help everyone to share your gifts of food, water and love with all.
Selfishness and greed leads to so much trouble on the earth.
Learn to love, sharing all God's gifts as your Creator intended.

Amen

TAKE EACH DAY

Great Spirit, help us to take each day as it comes:
To enjoy our animal companions and all of nature,
To honour the seasons and all that they bring,
To respect each other's pathways and to love one another.
We know deep in our hearts you are aware of all that happens,
That you constantly watch over us lovingly.
Life is energy and therefore eternal,
Our life on the earth is necessary for the soul to expand
In preparation for eternal life in spirit.
We humbly ask for courage to help us
Over any difficult times we may face while on earth.

Great Spirit, help us to think, speak and act
As you would wish us to.
Help us not to waste our precious spirit energy
On worry and negativity.
Keep us positive to face all of life's obstacles,
Bringing us close to you by acting only
For positivity and the light.

Amen

LIGHT AND LOVE

Great Spirit of light and love
We ask for the light of goodness to
Shine down through our homes
Into every dark corner,
To join the Christ light
Within each and everyone of us.

Help us through our development to
Join with each other in light and love.
We humbly ask this Great Spirit
So we may fight the dark forces together
Creating a planet of pure love and harmony.

Amen

ETERNAL PEACE

Our Lord,
Help keep our friends and loved ones safe from harm here on earth.
May they receive thy healing rays to help them through every day.

Friends and family in thy spirit world still need our prayers
To help them progress quickly through the etheric to Thy throne.

Please help them all, as we speak.
Then may we all be able to find eternal peace in our sleep.

Amen

WORLD PEACE

We humbly ask for help to release the love within
each of us, to flow freely among all countries.
Each country we know has different ways.
Let us learn patience with each other's ways.

Learn to tolerate another's views, for each person to unite in love
For the leaders of the world to give their love freely to one another.
This way we know is the true way forward.
Please, we ask for help for your wonderful gift of love to be shared
Freely among men for world peace.

Amen

BOUNTIFUL GOODS

Great Spirit,
Bountiful goods are given to mankind.
Help mankind to appreciate what has been given
With love from the Creator of all:

The beautiful earth and all she yields,
The animal kingdom, and our animal companions,
All of nature's realms.

Still the greed of mankind wants
More and more, destroying all around.
Help them stop and realise they need to care for these gifts
Before they destroy all, including themselves.

Amen

REINCARNATION

Every one of you will reincarnate
Until your spirit has accomplished
All of its mission successfully upon the earth.
Each one of you needs the teachings
That only life on earth can give.

HELP US TO HELP EACH OTHER

Gentle Jesus came to give us all love, compassion and healing.
He came to teach us how we should live,
To love each other, to have the basic virtues of life,
To be kind, true, gentle, loving unconditionally all,
To be tolerant, patient, honest,
To have respect for another and all the wisdom they have,
To be humble, peaceful and loyal to ourselves
To be able to support others also,
To share, to be generous
With our time, our love and understanding.
Help us now Father to help all souls
Who have forgotten why they came so long ago.
Give us help to do the same for all the souls that have gone astray.

Amen

HELP MANKIND

Dear God,
Please help all of mankind to wake up
To the fact that the earth has
Many life forms all equally
Entitled to live their lives happily as man does.

Help us all treat our fellow earthly companions
With the love and compassion they deserve.
Humans have to be woken up
To the fact that all life is precious,
All has been created by you to live together harmoniously.

Please let all people stop the senseless violence,
The cruelty to all types of life.
Let us all look after Mother Earth correctly, lovingly,
For all life which shares her.
We ask also that man treats fellow man
As he would wish himself to be treated.
Let us all be more humane,
So man can open his eyes and heart
To the beauty of all forms of life.

Dear God,
We thank you for listening to us
Whenever we pray to you,
And for sending us your love and help.

Amen

SOUNDS

How many truly listen to the beauty of bird song
Or the wind as it sings among the trees,
Or to water trickling in the brook,
Or chattering squirrels in the woodland.
These are the sounds of Creation that can heal our very soul.

So many prefer the sound of engines roaring,
Of music blaring and thumping out loud,
Or the sounds of people shouting at each other,
Yet nobody is really listening to anything.
Stop! Be silent and still.
Just simply experience what you are missing
Whilst the world is polluted with man-made sounds.

OPEN OUR HEARTS

Dear God let the hearts of our families, extended families, friends and acquaintances
Open to feel your unconditional love surround and embrace them.

Let their minds be opened wide so they can come to understand
The meaning of their life on earth.

Let their light glow brightly in understanding of the magnificent force of life- Love,
So they may live and breathe for one another.

Let them realise at last, that to give is to receive and to receive is to give.
Let us all have a greater understanding of spirit,
So we may fulfil all your wishes for us here on earth.

Amen

LOVE AND UNDERSTANDING

Dear Father, Mother God
We thank you for your gift of life.
Let us open to the Christ consciousness
Within us and live by your Truth.
Help us to give truth, love and understanding to all life.
Give us the strength to stand by our convictions
No matter what happens around us.
We thank the Spirit world for
Their love, guidance and patience
As all of us continue to make mistakes in our lives.
Thank you God for your love and understanding.

Amen

STRENGTH TO COPE

Our Father, Mother, who art in
Heaven, give us please the strength
To cope with our daily trials,
To look upon each other with kindly hearts.
Help us to see your light within
Each person we meet,
Not to pass any judgement of others.
To be charitable to all we meet.

Amen

NATURE'S REALMS

Sea life, large and small,
Birds, bees and insects,
Animal kingdom, wild and tame
Plants from the tiniest weed to the largest trees.
Flowers bright and pale,
We thank you Lord Creator of All
For these wondrous gifts you have given us.

Amen

STOP AND GIVE THANKS

Let us stop and give thanks to
God for sending us his son.
Remember all he taught us.
Start afresh today
Live life his way.
Let his earthly suffering
Not have been in vain.
We thank you God for all
You have given us.

Amen

THANKSGIVING

Our Father who has created all
We thank you for all our lives
Also for all the life on this
Beautiful planet that you have created for us.
Thank you for our parents, loved ones, children and friends.
May we also thank you for our loyal animal companions,
For the beautiful bird song that wakes us, especially in springtime.
Please inspire us all to clean up our planet, so that many more
Generations may live and enjoy this wonderful world.

Amen

EXTRA STRENGTH

Dear God
We ask for extra strength and protection be given for those
Who do rescue work in the rescue circles
Here on the earth plane and in the world of spirit.
Also extra love, strength and protection for those
Who help the lost wandering souls return to their home in the spirit world.
Please protect them all from any dark, deceiving evil forces they come across.
We ask that the all-empowering love-light, be sent to both sides.
Protect the whole Angelic Realm who help all continually,
All the innocent on all levels of our world.
We thank you God for your continued guidance in our lives.
Help us to listen to our inner God Spirit,
To learn to act upon inner consciousness.

Amen

COMPANIONS

When we look into the eyes of our animal companions,
Let us see their ever giving, ever loving innocent spirits
Within their earthly bodies.
Let us respect them by returning their unconditional love to
Them as they truly deserve with nothing else but our pure love.
They are always loyal, loving and true to us.
Never moody or changeable like their human companions.
Our dear animal companions who are so trustingly loyal,
Continually loving, can teach us all so very much about
How to live with one another.

Amen

HYMN TO CREATION

Great creator of all
We are in awe of all the great things you have created.
The world with its vast and varied plant life,
The life that flourishes beneath the river, streams, lakes and seas,
Our wonderful feathered birds in their bright plumes and colours,
All the animals of the enormous animal kingdom
Their individual beauty and mystery,
And the millions and millions of insects.

The Sun, Moon, Stars in the glorious Heavens, the Universes all around us.
What power, imagination and great love to create and provide for all.
We ask humbly for help to gain as much insight to all the forms of life.
To cherish, love and care for all around us, so our time on earth is not wasted.
It is our school where we can learn so much.

Let us not forget mankind and the beautiful shades, shapes and sizes we come in.
Let us not forget that we are all part of the Great Creator,
And we all have that tiny part of God within us.
Let us not forget we are all created from 'One' and are all part of the 'Whole One,'
God.

Amen

WHISPER

Every whisper in our ear
Every gentle brush of hair or touch upon the skin
A cobweb across our face
Each tell us a loved one who cares,
Has travelled from the world of Spirit to share a little of our time.
To show us how much they love and care,
They enclose us with their strength to help us through our days and nights.
We give thanks to God for the intermingling of the two worlds
So we are able to communicate with our dear ones.

Amen

PRAYER IN TIMES OF WAR

Father we humbly ask for help for all those in the war zones.
Please deliver the souls of the victims safely into your light.
Help all those who are bereaved through the consequences of the war.
Give all those involved extra love and healing to help them
Through the terrible time they are living through.
Please help them.
Stop them feeling bitter towards the world around them.
Let them know people are sending light by prayer to help them.
Conflicts in these areas are well under way,
Let the leaders of these countries come to their senses
And feel love towards the opposite side overwhelm them,
Making them unable to continue war of hate and greed.

Amen

PEACE AND EQUALITY

Dear God,
Help the world leaders see sense.
Give help to all countries in need.
Let the cost be forgotten and generosity of the well-fed wealthy help
The poorer hungry, homeless people of the world.
We know all have been catered for,
That ample for all mankind has been given by you God.
It is man's greed for wealth and power
That has upset your Divine plan to look after all your children equally.
For once, let all insist that help be given to those in need.
Let old debts be forgotten.

Dear God
We ask for help in this wish.
Let your light of goodness reach all, large and small, young and old.
Let people give freely with an open loving heart.
Help mankind awake from the madness of the world around.
We thank you Lord for listening to us.
We know we continually ask for help.
The power of love is here for us to send, we know Lord.
In your time we know all your children will awake,
All will have homes, food, water and clothes.
Peace and equality for all will be ours around the world.
Help us make them so, sooner rather than later God.

Amen

THE TRUE FOUNDATION OF ALL GOODNESS

Dear Mother/Father God, help us raise our thoughts away from our own selfish earthly wants and needs, let us humbly give you our total love and respect eternally.

Holy Mother/Father God, Creator of all mankind and all life, we your children honour that part of you within each and every one of us, we know you are always with us.

We your children are absorbed in love and trust for you, as you always provide for us and protect us from all evil, even when we may feel our world is falling apart and doubt may cross our minds.

We your children will be generous with unconditional love for all we meet and know, no matter what they may have done, as you God, forgive us all our mistakes, no judgement do you ever pass on us.

Help us to tread the path with Truth and Love, as Jesus your Son taught us when He came to earth to show us the right way to live, help us to keep temptation at bay.

Father/Mother God, we know you rule over all, that your goodness will always find a way through, as all life's trauma turns into a lesson for us to learn from, to aid our spiritual growth.

Let us look for the God light within all people, to be gentle, kind and master our emotions, to be able to look past all their earthly imperfections, to recognise we are all part of the 'Whole'. Help us to keep our faith strong as this is the true foundation of all Goodness in life.

Amen.

WORLDS

Dear Lord we thank you for every new morning and the learning each new day will bring us. We thank you for all who watch over us while we sleep.

We ask, Dear Father that all our families, loved ones and friends here on the earth and in the world of spirit, are given the Love and healing so they may step forward into Thy light.

We also humbly ask

> For the whole of mankind
> For the animal kingdom
> For our animal companions
> For the fish in the seas and rivers
> For the birds in the sky
> For all the plant kingdom
> For the nature spirits
> For the whole Angelic Realm
> For our Guardians and Guides
> For all those who help us from the unseen worlds around us,

That all we have mentioned receive the love, healing and light that they require for their daily lives and their highest good as they also progress along their spiritual journey.

Amen

FATHER/MOTHER GOD

Dear Father/Mother God
Your Son Jesus Christ
Taught us, 'Love thy neighbour as thyself',
Taught us not to seek glamour and self glorification.
So many of us have forgotten our Master's words that
Selfishness is the norm here on earth.

Dear Father/Mother God
Teach us how to help others understand the needs of our inner spirit,
To give service in Love and Truth to all God's creatures.
Help us to show others how the happiness gained from self gratification
Is so very short lived.

Dear Father/Mother God,
Help us to show others the lasting joy there is through service and the giving of self,
To live the way your Son has taught us.

Amen

GUIDANCE HOME

Mother/ Father God awaits you,
Watching each step you take.
Encouraging you from within to
Leave your problems to them.

Peace within you all please,
There is no need to worry
All has been planned
For each of you, so long ago.

Leave your worries,
Dry those tears,
Live life to the full,
Gaining all the wisdom you can.

This is God's wish,
For your spirit to grow
For your mind expand and
All avenues to explore.

Climb the golden ladder
Without looking down.
Step up, go on forward
Without allowing fear to encompass your soul.

Guardian Angels watch over you
Never letting you fall.
Look up to the love- light
That is guiding you home.

EVERY NIGHT

Every night as the dark velvet veil encloses us,
Beautiful stars shine down on us.

Let all here on earth burn our inner Christ Light,
Just as brightly as the stars.

So all the Universe may see our light twinkle from afar,
Sparkling with the Love of Our Creator within us.

LET US GIVE THANKS

How often do we wake and take each day for granted,
To sleep and to wake to a new day,
A new world?
We have our families, friends, neighbours, clothes, food, and our homes,
But do we remember to thank the Lord?

God sends us His unconditional love every night and day
He gives us the means to grow our food,
Manufacture our clothes and all our material goods.
Do we give thanks to the Lord?

We take every day everything it gives us,
Perhaps without even a thought for our Father/Mother God,
What ungrateful children we are.
Let us give thanks, every morning, every evening,
Every second of each day, to our Mother/Father God.

Let us give thanks for all we have
And for the Love flowing from our Creator's Heart,
To each one of us each day.

Amen

WE THANK YOU GOD

We thank you God for all we have,
Our lives, our families, our clothes, our homes, and our jobs,
For all the people we meet each day,

We give thanks for the Love and Guidance our Guides and Helpers give us,
For the healings we receive from you dear God, through all the Angelic Realms.

We thank you God for our wonderful world, and all life's opportunities,
So we may grow to be nearer to you, dear Lord,
Each moment of each day.

Amen

LIFE IN THE FAST LANE

Rush, rush, no time to stop awhile.

Hurry, hurry, your lives are in the fast lane.

Faster, you all go, doing far too much, bringing disease among you, within you too.

No time to relax or unwind, to recharge your body, spirit and soul.

Stop, reconnect with your Maker.

Remember the Creator, who created all of you and every living spirit.

He gave you the things you see, hear, feel, also the food you eat and water to quench your thirst.

The world and the universe, are all His creation.

Still you have no time to give thanks for all of this.

Take that much needed time for self, go into the peace within.

Give your thanks for your life, your families and friends, for all you have.

Be grateful for your life, and all it brings each and every day.

God loves you all, be at peace with the Divine One.

Once you have found God again, you will wonder why you ever left.

That peace you need so much will be yours at last.

Faith brings you the love, truth and peace you all yearn and search for.

Your Father/Mother God longs for the return of his lost children.

The Creator God's love for you never dies.

Breathe in the breath of God, breathe out peace to all.

Reconnect in love with your Mother/Father God. You have nothing to lose but so much to gain.

DEAR FRIENDS

Dear friends, we here in the Spirit World, wish to thank you for reading our words to you. We know it is not always easy for you in your world. We hope these spiritual truths help you on your pathway through life's problems. Enjoy your world. It is a beautiful world that God has given you all.

Give thanks each day to your God in prayer. Prayer does not mean you have to go to a place of worship. We have mentioned that you all have the Christ Spirit within you. Your bodies are your personal temples. Take a few moments each day to sit quietly with your own spiritual self, to listen to your tiny part of God. Embrace your God with love and thanks each and every day.

May we leave you with the Blessing of your Mother/Father Creator's Love.

Printed in the United Kingdom
by Lightning Source UK Ltd.
R607500001B/R6075PG115497UKSX1B/1-45